# Supporting Relationships and Friendships

## Knowledge and Skills for Social Care Workers Series

The *Knowledge and Skills for Social Care Workers* series features accessible and interactive open learning workbooks which tackle a range of key subjects relevant to people working with adults in residential or domiciliary settings. Topics covered in this series include how social care workers can communicate effectively, health and safety, safeguarding adults from harm and abuse and supporting relationships and friendships.

*other books in the series*

**Supporting Positive Behaviour**
**A Workbook for Social Care Workers**
*Suzan Collins*
ISBN 978 1 84905 073 9

**Effective Communication**
**A Workbook for Social Care Workers**
*Suzan Collins*
ISBN 978 1 84310 027 3

**Safeguarding Adults**
**A Workbook for Social Care Workers**
*Suzan Collins*
ISBN 978 1 84310 928 0

**Health and Safety**
**A Workbook for Social Care Workers**
*Suzan Collins*
ISBN 978 1 84310 929 7

**Reflecting On and Developing Your Practice**
**A Workbook for Social Care Workers**
*Suzan Collins*
ISBN 978 1 84310 930 3

# Supporting Relationships and Friendships

## A Workbook for Social Care Workers

### Suzan Collins

Jessica Kingsley Publishers
London and Philadelphia

First published in 2010
by Jessica Kingsley Publishers
116 Pentonville Road
London N1 9JB, UK
and
400 Market Street, Suite 400
Philadelphia, PA 19106, USA

*www.jkp.com*

**Library of Congress Cataloging in Publication Data**
Collins, Suzan, 1960-
    Supporting relationships and friendships : a workbook for social care workers / Suzan
Collins.
        p. cm.
    Includes bibliographical references.
    ISBN 978-1-84905-072-2 (alk. paper)
    1. Friendship. 2. Social work with older people. I. Title.
    BF575.F66C645 2010
    361.3'2--dc22

                                                2010000318

**British Library Cataloguing in Publication Data**
A CIP catalogue record for this book is available from the British Library

ISBN 978 1 84905 072 2

Printed and bound by
MPG Books Limited

# Acknowledgements

I would like to thank the following people for their advice and support:

Anne Earley, Assistant Home Leader, Aspects and Milestones Trust,
Andrew Williams, Scheme Manager, Care and Support, East Living,
Janet Elliott, Safeguarding Adults Lead, Primary Care Trust and
Cheryl Able, Registered Home Manager, Lilac Lodge and Lavender Cottage.

People who gave permission to be photographed and to use these
photographs in this workbook are:

Vida Kwatemaa, Nicola Jackson, Oyetola Makanjuola,
Jamal Ahmed and Enrico Bareggi

Maslow's Hierarchy of Needs, p.17: all reasonable efforts to trace the copyright
holder have been made, and any queries should be addressed to the publishers.

This workbook meets the requirements of the following standards, guidance and qualifications:

Care Quality Commission (CQC)
Care Home for Adults Standards 6, 7, 10, 12 and 15
Care Home for Older People Standards 7, 10, 12 and 13

General Social Care Council (GSCC)
Code of Practice Standards 1, 2, 3, 4 and 5

Skills for Care (SFC)
Common Induction Standard (CIS) 1

# Contents

# Introduction

People receiving community care services – care in residential services or in their own homes – want friendships and relationships, just like any other person, and are at greater risk of feeling isolated. This workbook will equip social care staff with the knowledge and skills to understand what friendships and relationships mean to service users' health and well-being.

*Supporting Relationships and Friendships* looks at how to assess social skills and the qualities needed in a friend. Sharing interests can provide companionship and self-esteem, but some friendships can become negative or burdensome, and this book offers useful guidance on supporting service users in managing their friendships and relationships.

Everyone has a right to have relationships and this workbook looks at how you can promote a proactive and positive approach in supporting service users in developing and maintaining social, personal and sexual relationships and how this can be supported while balancing the potential risks, thus protecting the people you support from potential harm and/or exploitation.

## ABOUT THIS BOOK

This workbook will provide guidance on supporting friendships and relationships; however, your organization will have its own policies and procedures in place for you to follow.

It is not always possible for staff to be taken off the rota to attend a training course and so this workbook has been devised. It uses a variety of training methods:

- reading passages where you will expand your knowledge
- completing exercises
- completing a self-assessment tool which shows you the knowledge you have acquired.

As a social care worker, you have to work to certain standards, which are set out by various professional bodies. This workbook links to several standards and in case you are not familiar with them, here is a brief explanation about each one.

*Skills for Care* (SfC) has a set of standards called Common Induction Standards which apply to all new staff in the care sector (except those who are supporting people with learning disabilities, who will need to complete the Learning Disability Qualification Induction Award). The Common Induction Standards and the Learning Disability Qualification Induction Award should be completed within three months of being in post. This workbook meets the requirements of the Common Induction Standard 1.

*Care Quality Commission* (CQC) took over the work of the Commission for Social Care Inspection (CSCI) on 1 April 2009 (it also took over the work of the Healthcare Commission and the Mental Health Act Commission). The CQC has sets of standards for you and your workplace to meet. There are different sets of standards and it will depend on where you work as to which standards you need to work to. If you are unsure, please ask your manager. This workbook meets the requirements of Care Home for Adults Standards 6, 7, 10, 12 and 15, and Care Home for Older People Standards 7, 10, 12 and 13; reference to these standards are made in this workbook.

*General Social Care Council* (GSCC) has a Code of Practice with six standards that reflect good practice. This workbook meets parts of the requirements for Standards 1, 2, 3, 4 and 5.

Towards the end of the workbook you will be asked to complete a self-assessment questionnaire on what you have learnt from completing this workbook. Once you have completed this, your manager or trainer will complete the certificate on pp.107–108 and give it to you. You will then have completed training on supporting relationships and friendships.

I hope that you find this a useful workbook and wish you well in your career.

This workbook can be:

- read straight through from front to back

- used as a reference book.

In this workbook, I have referred to the people you support as 'service users' and 'he/him' rather than continually writing he/she him/her.

Name of Learner:. . . . . . . . . . . . . . . . . . . . . . . . . . . . Date: . . . . . . . . . . . . .

Signature of Learner:. . . . . . . . . . . . . . . . . . . . . . . Date: . . . . . . . . . . . . .

Name of Manager or Trainer:. . . . . . . . . . . . . . . . . . . . . . . . . . . . . . . . . . . .

Signature of Manager or Trainer: . . . . . . . . . . . . . . . Date: . . . . . . . . . . . . .

Workplace address or name of organization:

. . . . . . . . . . . . . . . . . . . . . . . . . . . . . . . . . . . . . . . . . . . . . . . . . . . . . . . . . .

. . . . . . . . . . . . . . . . . . . . . . . . . . . . . . . . . . . . . . . . . . . . . . . . . . . . . . . . . .

. . . . . . . . . . . . . . . . . . . . . . . . . . . . . . . . . . . . . . . . . . . . . . . . . . . . . . . . . .

. . . . . . . . . . . . . . . . . . . . . . . . . . . . . . . . . . . . . . . . . . . . . . . . . . . . . . . . . .

# Responsibilities

Everyone who is supporting a person in the care setting has responsibilities, and it will depend on the position the person holds as to what their responsibilities are.

## MANAGERS' RESPONSIBILITIES

Social care employers must:

- Make sure people are suitable to enter the workforce and understand their roles and responsibilities;

- Have written policies and procedures in place to enable social care workers to meet the General Social Care Council (GSCC) Code of Practice for Social Care Workers;

- Provide training and development opportunities to enable social care workers to strengthen and develop their skills and knowledge;

- Put in place and implement written policies and procedures to deal with dangerous, discriminatory or exploitative behaviour and practice; and

- Promote the GSCC's code of practice to social care workers, service users and carers and co-operate with the GSCC's proceedings. (GSCC 2002)

Social care employers must provide written guidance and this will be in the form of:

- Care plans, support plans and/or health action plans

- Risk assessments (if appropriate)

'Care homes will develop policies, procedures and/or codes of practice, appropriate to the setting, on sexuality and relationships' (CQC Care Home for Adults Appendix 2 Policies and Procedures).

The arrangements for health and personal care ensure that service user's privacy and dignity are respected at all times, and with particular regard to maintaining social contacts with relatives and friends. (CQC Care Home for Adults Standard 10)

## SOCIAL CARE WORKERS' RESPONSIBILITIES

Social care workers must:

- Protect the rights and promote the interests of service users and carers;
- Strive to establish and maintain the trust and confidence of service users and carers;
- Promote the independence of service users while protecting them as far as possible from danger or harm;
- Respect the rights of service users while seeking to ensure that their behaviour does not harm themselves or other people;
- Uphold public trust and confidence in social care services; and
- Be accountable for the quality of their work and take responsibility for maintaining and improving their knowledge and skills. (GSCC 2002)

As a social care worker, you should:

- follow your job description
- read, understand and follow policies, procedures and risk assessments (you will read more about risk assessments on pp.61–62)
- promote the rights of the people you support.

## CQC Care Home for Adults Standards

**15.1:** Staff support service users to maintain family links and friendships inside and outside the home, subject to restrictions agreed in the individual Plan and Contract (subject to Standards 2 and 6 if necessary).

**15.2:** Family and friends are welcomed, and their involvement in daily routines and activities is encouraged, with the service user's agreement.

**15.3:** Service users choose whom they see and when; and can see visitors in their rooms and in private.

**15.4:** Service users have opportunities to meet people and make friends who do not have their disability/illness/addiction.

**15.5:** Service users can develop and maintain intimate personal relationships with people of their choice, and information and specialist guidance are provided to help the service user to make appropriate decisions.

## CQC Care Home for Older People Standards

**13.2:** Service users are able to receive visitors in private.

**13.3:** Service users choose whom they see and do not see.

✍ Does your organization have policies and procedures on supporting relationships and friendships?                    Yes/No

Whether you answered 'Yes' or 'No', please say how this affects what you do or do not do.

. . . . . . . . . . . . . . . . . . . . . . . . . . . . . . . . . . . . . . . . . . . . . . . . . . . . .

. . . . . . . . . . . . . . . . . . . . . . . . . . . . . . . . . . . . . . . . . . . . . . . . . . . . .

. . . . . . . . . . . . . . . . . . . . . . . . . . . . . . . . . . . . . . . . . . . . . . . . . . . . .

## SERVICE USERS' RESPONSIBILITIES

Service users should:

- avoid knowingly putting themselves and/or others at risk
- contribute wherever possible to their risk assessment and work with services to reduce and minimize risks.

# What is Friendship?

Before we can support others who want to develop new friendships or relationships, or maintain existing ones, we need to look first at what a friend is and what makes a person a friend rather than someone we meet on a daily basis, perhaps at the bus stop or at the post office counter etc.

The definition of a friend from a Collins dictionary is: 'A person known well to another and regarded with liking, affection and loyalty'.

✎ Do you agree with this definition? Yes/No

If you have answered 'No', please explain:

. . . . . . . . . . . . . . . . . . . . . . . . . . . . . . . . . . . . . . . . . . . . . . . . . .

. . . . . . . . . . . . . . . . . . . . . . . . . . . . . . . . . . . . . . . . . . . . . . . . . .

. . . . . . . . . . . . . . . . . . . . . . . . . . . . . . . . . . . . . . . . . . . . . . . . . .

People will often think of a good friend as someone who offers support and understanding – who is loyal, caring and always willing to listen and help, even during difficult times. An important part of friendship is the fact that it should be mutual, so this book explores not only how to find a friend, but also the skills to be a good friend.

Building new friendships and relationships and maintaining old ones can:

- help friends to get through a bad experience or a difficult period of time

- enhance self-esteem

- provide practical support.

✎ Take some time here to think of two of your friends. How did they become a friend, rather than someone you just meet now and again? What is special about them for you to want them as friends? Why not have them just as acquaintances?

. . . . . . . . . . . . . . . . . . . . . . . . . . . . . . . . . . . . . . . . . . . . . . . . . .

. . . . . . . . . . . . . . . . . . . . . . . . . . . . . . . . . . . . . . . . . . . . . . . . . .

. . . . . . . . . . . . . . . . . . . . . . . . . . . . . . . . . . . . . . . . . . . . . . . . . .

Think about the difference between the friendship you have with each of them and the relationship you have with your mum or dad. Then, think about whether a service user may feel as though staff watch or judge him in a way that parents might. It is likely that they will sometimes, as there are times when you need to assess what the service user is doing, how he does it etc.

What is the difference, for the service user, between having a friendship with a friend and the relationship the service user has with you? While you can be friendly with a service user, you also have a professional relationship – something which is explored in greater detail on pp.59–60.

Now think about friendship and service users. People living by themselves can have an active social life and be happy, but others may not have a social life and may be lonely. Service users can even live in a small or large residential or nursing home with lots of people and still feel lonely.

Years ago many people who required care and support lived in institutional-like settings where there were regimes, no choice of what to eat or wear, loss of identity and probably very limited contact with the outside world. Therefore, it would not have been easy or possible for people who were in these settings to meet new people and, if a service user did meet a new person, they may not have had the social skills to know what to say, what behaviour was acceptable, etc. Nowadays things have changed, and any service users who wants a friendship or relationship should be supported in their decisions.

✍ Ask yourself these questions:

Can all service users have friends? What if a service user has profound learning or physical disabilities or cannot speak, or has challenging behaviour, or mental health needs, or is an older person?

. . . . . . . . . . . . . . . . . . . . . . . . . . . . . . . . . . . . . . . . . . . . . . . . .

. . . . . . . . . . . . . . . . . . . . . . . . . . . . . . . . . . . . . . . . . . . . . . . . .

. . . . . . . . . . . . . . . . . . . . . . . . . . . . . . . . . . . . . . . . . . . . . . . . .

How will I know if a service user wants or needs a friend, particularly if they have limited communication?

. . . . . . . . . . . . . . . . . . . . . . . . . . . . . . . . . . . . . . . . . . . . . . . . .

. . . . . . . . . . . . . . . . . . . . . . . . . . . . . . . . . . . . . . . . . . . . . . . . .

. . . . . . . . . . . . . . . . . . . . . . . . . . . . . . . . . . . . . . . . . . . . . . . . .

How do I start the process of developing friendships?

. . . . . . . . . . . . . . . . . . . . . . . . . . . . . . . . . . . . . . . . . . . . . . . . .

. . . . . . . . . . . . . . . . . . . . . . . . . . . . . . . . . . . . . . . . . . . . . . . . .

. . . . . . . . . . . . . . . . . . . . . . . . . . . . . . . . . . . . . . . . . . . . . . . . .

This workbook should help you to answer these questions and guide you on what you need to do to support service users.

## FRIENDSHIP AND SERVICE USERS' NEEDS

We all have needs, and fulfilling these needs can help us to develop as humans. Service users have needs, just like anybody else, but you may need to take some time to establish what their needs are. You can't tell if a service user wants or needs a friend unless the service user tells you. Some service users may not tell you as they may be embarrassed or assume that staff in a residential home help with personal care and nothing else.

To find out their needs, you can ask the service user or you could use a model like Maslow's 'Hierarchy of Needs' as a way of opening a conversation about their opinions on what they want and what they need. If it is not possible to do this with the service user you could do it with a relative, friend, advocate, etc. The diagram is based on a theory in psychology that Abraham Maslow proposed in his 1943 paper 'A theory of human motivation'. As you can see, it has five levels to it.

According to Maslow, until the two bottom lines are achieved, it is unlikely that you can move on and develop. Therefore, you need to look at how you can provide the service user with the right support before they can achieve the other levels or sections and reach self-actualization (assuming these have not been reached yet).

✍ Looking at Maslow's Hierarchy of Needs, which are being met in your place of work?

. . . . . . . . . . . . . . . . . . . . . . . . . . . . . . . . . . . . . . . . . . . . . . . . . . . . . . . .

. . . . . . . . . . . . . . . . . . . . . . . . . . . . . . . . . . . . . . . . . . . . . . . . . . . . . . . .

. . . . . . . . . . . . . . . . . . . . . . . . . . . . . . . . . . . . . . . . . . . . . . . . . . . . . . . .

## HOW TO MEET SERVICE USERS' NEEDS

A Community Care Assessment can help to identify some care needs and this may cover only the first two stages of Maslow's hierarchy.

To reach the personal development and growth stage (the top level of the hierarchy on p.17), you will need to enable the people you support to learn new things and achieve. This can be anything from learning to prepare a snack, vacuum a carpet, swim, read or write to learning how to catch a bus, to getting a job, watering the plants or participating in a reminiscence group etc. To achieve status and recognition, we all need a role or two and when we carry out these roles people thank us and appreciate us.

To arrive at social fulfilment, things that can help include belonging to a group (provide support if the service user expresses a desire to join a group). Groups can be involved in a range of interests, for example, doing voluntary work, playing in a pool team in the pub, joining a knitting circle, playing cards or dominoes, joining a reading circle or working on an allotment.

Social fulfilment can also be found through activities, love and friendship – you will see by completing some exercises later in this workbook what the service user can do during the day/evening and if he has friends etc. We all need to have friends and we all need to be loved.

✍ If your place of work is not supporting service users to meet any of the higher levels, what can you do about it?

. . . . . . . . . . . . . . . . . . . . . . . . . . . . . . . . . . . . . . . . . . . . . . . . . . . . . . . .

. . . . . . . . . . . . . . . . . . . . . . . . . . . . . . . . . . . . . . . . . . . . . . . . . . . . . . . .

. . . . . . . . . . . . . . . . . . . . . . . . . . . . . . . . . . . . . . . . . . . . . . . . . . . . . . . .

✍ If the individual has not met all the levels of the hierarchy, how will this affect his/her self-esteem and independence?

. . . . . . . . . . . . . . . . . . . . . . . . . . . . . . . . . . . . . . . . . . . . . . . . . . . . . . . .

. . . . . . . . . . . . . . . . . . . . . . . . . . . . . . . . . . . . . . . . . . . . . . . . . . . . . . . .

. . . . . . . . . . . . . . . . . . . . . . . . . . . . . . . . . . . . . . . . . . . . . . . . . . . . . . . .

## DOES A SERVICE USER WANT A FRIENDSHIP OR RELATIONSHIP?

Before thinking about how to help a service user to develop a new friendship, first think carefully about whether or not they want a friendship. As a member of staff supporting the service user, it is important that you do not put pressure on the person to do anything that they do not want to do, or in which they have no interest.

Not all people who have a learning disability or mental health need or who are elderly will require help in making friends or maintaining them. Many people have good social skills and social opportunities to develop friends without any help. However, there will be some people who may find at times during their life that they want more people in it.

Moving into a residential home can sometimes mean that the service users lose close contact with family and friends and this can result in a feeling that they have lost a part of their history unless you help. It will depend on the individual as to how much help and support the person requires.

It is important that you read the support plan and find out if support is required and, if it is, consider:

- the level of support required

- support by whom

- the kind of relationship the service user wants: friend, companion or sexual partner?

There will be areas in the support plan that you may want to follow up to enable a person you support to have a friend or maintain an existing friendship.

In some circumstances it may be important to discuss your ideas with your manager in the first instance and he/she will decide who else can make a valuable contribution (in terms of support); this will also ensure that everyone is working consistently to support the individual.

I have heard some staff in the past say that the 'service users don't need friends as we are paid to look after the service users'. This is incorrect: staff are paid to support the service users.

✍ Can you see that this assumption is wrong?                Yes/No

If you have answered 'No', please justify your answer

. . . . . . . . . . . . . . . . . . . . . . . . . . . . . . . . . . . . . . . . . . . . . . . . . .

. . . . . . . . . . . . . . . . . . . . . . . . . . . . . . . . . . . . . . . . . . . . . . . . . .

. . . . . . . . . . . . . . . . . . . . . . . . . . . . . . . . . . . . . . . . . . . . . . . . . .

✍ Think of a person you support (but do not use names or initials here as you do not want to breach confidentiality).

Does the person already have friends and keeps in touch or sees them regularly?                    Yes/No

If you have answered 'No' to the above, what can you do about it?

. . . . . . . . . . . . . . . . . . . . . . . . . . . . . . . . . . . . . . . . . . . . . . . . . . . . .

. . . . . . . . . . . . . . . . . . . . . . . . . . . . . . . . . . . . . . . . . . . . . . . . . . . . .

. . . . . . . . . . . . . . . . . . . . . . . . . . . . . . . . . . . . . . . . . . . . . . . . . . . . .

Does the person have friends but has not heard from them for a long while?                    Yes/No

If you have answered 'Yes' to the above, what can you do about it?

. . . . . . . . . . . . . . . . . . . . . . . . . . . . . . . . . . . . . . . . . . . . . . . . . . . . .

. . . . . . . . . . . . . . . . . . . . . . . . . . . . . . . . . . . . . . . . . . . . . . . . . . . . .

. . . . . . . . . . . . . . . . . . . . . . . . . . . . . . . . . . . . . . . . . . . . . . . . . . . . .

✍ Is there a limit to how many friends a person can have?                    Yes/No

If you have answered 'Yes', please explain:

. . . . . . . . . . . . . . . . . . . . . . . . . . . . . . . . . . . . . . . . . . . . . . . . . . . . .

. . . . . . . . . . . . . . . . . . . . . . . . . . . . . . . . . . . . . . . . . . . . . . . . . . . . .

. . . . . . . . . . . . . . . . . . . . . . . . . . . . . . . . . . . . . . . . . . . . . . . . . . . . .

✍ Does the service user want or need a friend?                    Yes/No

If you have answered 'Yes' to the above, what can you do about it?

. . . . . . . . . . . . . . . . . . . . . . . . . . . . . . . . . . . . . . . . . . . . . . . . . . . . .

. . . . . . . . . . . . . . . . . . . . . . . . . . . . . . . . . . . . . . . . . . . . . . . . . . . . .

. . . . . . . . . . . . . . . . . . . . . . . . . . . . . . . . . . . . . . . . . . . . . . . . . . . . .

✍ What is the difference between wanting a friend and needing a friend?

Wanting means:

. . . . . . . . . . . . . . . . . . . . . . . . . . . . . . . . . . . . . . . . . . . . . . . . . . . . .

. . . . . . . . . . . . . . . . . . . . . . . . . . . . . . . . . . . . . . . . . . . . . . . . . . . . .

. . . . . . . . . . . . . . . . . . . . . . . . . . . . . . . . . . . . . . . . . . . . . . . . . . . . .

Needing means:

. . . . . . . . . . . . . . . . . . . . . . . . . . . . . . . . . . . . . . . . . . . . . . . . . . . . . .

. . . . . . . . . . . . . . . . . . . . . . . . . . . . . . . . . . . . . . . . . . . . . . . . . . . . . .

. . . . . . . . . . . . . . . . . . . . . . . . . . . . . . . . . . . . . . . . . . . . . . . . . . . . . .

## SUGGESTIONS FOR FINDING OUT WHETHER A SERVICE USER WANTS A FRIEND

It can be difficult to find out whether someone wants a friend. As mentioned earlier, you could use Maslow's diagram as a way of opening a conversation about general needs, and bring in friendship as one of these.

What you must not do is to say something along the lines of, 'You haven't got any friends and you need some, I will help you...'

Try to broach the subject in general, everyday conversations with the person you support. You will be listening and picking up on who he mentions and if he has friends, if he is happy with them or if he would like different or new friends.

You may be supporting people who have very limited communication skills and you may not be able to have a verbal conversation. If the person can use different forms of communication, e.g. Makaton, picture boards, photographs or something similar, you can have a discussion using these. If the person's communication is extremely limited, you can pick up from his body language or maybe by showing the person a photograph and if he smiles he is showing that he is happy. If you would like to know how to communicate effectively, you will find another workbook in this series, *Effective Communication*, useful.

It is advantageous for the service user to have some method of communication such as Makaton or, using objects to communicate, for example holding up a cup to say he wants a cup of tea or pointing to a picture of the pub, perhaps to say he would like to go there. We say a lot with our bodies, e.g. smiling, winking, and some people use this to communicate.

## EXISTING SOCIAL NETWORKS

Another way to find out if a service user wants or needs a friend is to look at who is in the person's life at the moment. The people you support will have a range of different kinds of contacts, only some of whom will be friends. They will include:

- Friends
- Acquaintances: people who you have casual contact with and see now and again
- Enablers: people who will enable the service user to do something
- Advocates: people who can empower service users so their voices are heard
- Volunteers: people who will enable the service user to do something, such as attend college or go to the cinema. It may not be in the volunteer's remit to help the service user build a friendship unless this is specifically asked for, but if it is, the volunteer can support the service user in his chosen activity and encourage or facilitate the service user to build bonds with people.

Being a social care worker you do not know everything about the service user and therefore you and the service user may have to ask others about who the service user is close to, speaks to or smiles at. This may be parents, relatives, day service staff or staff at groups that the service user attends.

You may find that the service user's existing friends arrive at the home while you are present. The service user may have friends at the college or day service who have never been invited to the home. If this is the case, what can you do about it?

✎ Tick the people who you know are in the service user's life:

| People in the service users life | ✓ |
|---|---|
| Paid staff | |
| People who say they are the service user's friends but do not see each other regularly | |
| Relatives | |
| Relatives and/or friends who live locally | |
| Relatives and/or frends who live far away | |
| A person sharing a sexual relationship | |
| People who have a learning and/or physical disability or mental health need | |
| People who do not have a learning and/or physical disability or mental health need | |
| No one other than staff | |

## FAMILIES AND FRIENDSHIPS

While we often think of families and friends separately, our family are often also our friends. The relationship the service user has with his family and the relationship the family has with the service user can change when a service user is in residential care, and it is worth being aware of potential difficulties and trying to support the service user wherever possible.

Here are some examples of issues which I have seen cause problems for service users:

- A service user with dementia who is a mother starts to fulfil the role of a 'child' in her family, with her daughter playing the mothering role.

- A relative may not want to visit the service user either because the service user has changed and grown in confidence, becoming more independent, or because the relative does not like what he has become – he may be frightened to visit as the service user seems to be a different person to who he used to be.

✎ In some cases the only people in the service user's life are paid staff and one of the reasons for this could be because the service user has not been supported to keep in touch with their family and friends. What can you do to increase the number of people in the service user's life who are not paid staff?

. . . . . . . . . . . . . . . . . . . . . . . . . . . . . . . . . . . . . . . . . . . . . . . . . .

. . . . . . . . . . . . . . . . . . . . . . . . . . . . . . . . . . . . . . . . . . . . . . . . . .

. . . . . . . . . . . . . . . . . . . . . . . . . . . . . . . . . . . . . . . . . . . . . . . . . .

✍ Has the service user ever commented on there being more
staff in his life than anyone else?                                   Yes/No

If so, has the service user told you what he wants you to do about this? Yes/No
If you have answered 'Yes', what is it he wants you to do?

. . . . . . . . . . . . . . . . . . . . . . . . . . . . . . . . . . . . . . . . . . . . . . . . . . . . . . . . . .

. . . . . . . . . . . . . . . . . . . . . . . . . . . . . . . . . . . . . . . . . . . . . . . . . . . . . . . . . .

. . . . . . . . . . . . . . . . . . . . . . . . . . . . . . . . . . . . . . . . . . . . . . . . . . . . . . . . . .

✍ If the service user is unable to comment on the number of staff in his life,
what can you do about it?

. . . . . . . . . . . . . . . . . . . . . . . . . . . . . . . . . . . . . . . . . . . . . . . . . . . . . . . . . .

. . . . . . . . . . . . . . . . . . . . . . . . . . . . . . . . . . . . . . . . . . . . . . . . . . . . . . . . . .

. . . . . . . . . . . . . . . . . . . . . . . . . . . . . . . . . . . . . . . . . . . . . . . . . . . . . . . . . .

✍ If the opportunities were there, can the service user make
friends without you?                                                 Yes/No

How do you know?

. . . . . . . . . . . . . . . . . . . . . . . . . . . . . . . . . . . . . . . . . . . . . . . . . . . . . . . . . .

. . . . . . . . . . . . . . . . . . . . . . . . . . . . . . . . . . . . . . . . . . . . . . . . . . . . . . . . . .

✍ Does the service user want the same qualities in his friends as
you do in yours?                                                     Yes/No

How do you know?

. . . . . . . . . . . . . . . . . . . . . . . . . . . . . . . . . . . . . . . . . . . . . . . . . . . . . . . . . .

. . . . . . . . . . . . . . . . . . . . . . . . . . . . . . . . . . . . . . . . . . . . . . . . . . . . . . . . . .

✍ Does the service user want friends who are people with a disability,
people without a disability or both?

. . . . . . . . . . . . . . . . . . . . . . . . . . . . . . . . . . . . . . . . . . . . . . . . . . . . . . . . . .

. . . . . . . . . . . . . . . . . . . . . . . . . . . . . . . . . . . . . . . . . . . . . . . . . . . . . . . . . .

How do you know?

. . . . . . . . . . . . . . . . . . . . . . . . . . . . . . . . . . . . . . . . . . . . . . . . . . . . . . . . . .

. . . . . . . . . . . . . . . . . . . . . . . . . . . . . . . . . . . . . . . . . . . . . . . . . . . . . . . . . .

# Friendship and Social Skills

To have a friend means that you need to be a friend to the other person and you will need qualities and social skills to do this. Below are some examples of qualities you might expect to find in a friend.

✍ Please ask the service user if possible to tick the ones he is able to do or do this exercise on his behalf.

| Qualities of a friend | ✓ |
|---|---|
| I can do things for the other person | |
| I can keep a secret | |
| I am loyal | |
| I can take advice | |
| I am interested in the other person's well-being | |
| I will help when needed | |
| I will understand if the other person makes a mistake | |

| | |
|---|---|
| I can be supportive when things are going well | |
| I can be supportive when things are not going well | |
| I will listen to the other person | |

✎ Having completed this exercise, what does it tell you?

. . . . . . . . . . . . . . . . . . . . . . . . . . . . . . . . . . . . . . . . . . . . . . . . . . . . . . . .

. . . . . . . . . . . . . . . . . . . . . . . . . . . . . . . . . . . . . . . . . . . . . . . . . . . . . . . .

. . . . . . . . . . . . . . . . . . . . . . . . . . . . . . . . . . . . . . . . . . . . . . . . . . . . . . . .

✎ Does anything need to be done?                                    Yes/No

If you answered 'Yes', please say what you can do about it.

. . . . . . . . . . . . . . . . . . . . . . . . . . . . . . . . . . . . . . . . . . . . . . . . . . . . . . . .

. . . . . . . . . . . . . . . . . . . . . . . . . . . . . . . . . . . . . . . . . . . . . . . . . . . . . . . .

. . . . . . . . . . . . . . . . . . . . . . . . . . . . . . . . . . . . . . . . . . . . . . . . . . . . . . . .

✎ What does the service user want from the friendship?

. . . . . . . . . . . . . . . . . . . . . . . . . . . . . . . . . . . . . . . . . . . . . . . . . . . . . . . .

. . . . . . . . . . . . . . . . . . . . . . . . . . . . . . . . . . . . . . . . . . . . . . . . . . . . . . . .

. . . . . . . . . . . . . . . . . . . . . . . . . . . . . . . . . . . . . . . . . . . . . . . . . . . . . . . .

## SOCIAL SKILLS

Developing or maintaining a friendship can be hard work, but it can become easier if you possess good social skills. Social skills help you to interact and communicate successfully with others. They include being able to empathize with others, to observe common social rules and behaviours, and to understand both verbal and non-verbal communication.

Social skills can be affected by your cognitive ability: if you acquire knowledge and information in a different way to others, or if you perceive and think about things in a different way, then it can make friendship more difficult. This can be applicable to people with various kinds of autism and people with various kinds of dementia.

It is also about how we interact with our surroundings and how we act and behave in front of others.

These social skills are important and are needed in a reciprocal friendship or relationship to gain acceptance from others. If we do not have these skills then we may be unable to have a friendship or relationship or it may be rocky and unstable. We all need these skills, not just people with a learning disability, a mental health need or who are elderly.

✍ What will happen to the people you support if they do not learn, maintain or use these social skills and/or have people to provide support in these situations?

. . . . . . . . . . . . . . . . . . . . . . . . . . . . . . . . . . . . . . . . . . . . . . .

. . . . . . . . . . . . . . . . . . . . . . . . . . . . . . . . . . . . . . . . . . . . . . .

. . . . . . . . . . . . . . . . . . . . . . . . . . . . . . . . . . . . . . . . . . . . . . .

I suspect your answer included that the people you support may be socially excluded and/or feel isolated.

When you were growing up, you were taught social skills by your family and learnt from your own experiences how to make friends. You also learnt how to behave from people's reactions and watching others. Can you remember it?

I do not remember my early years well but I do remember playing in the playground with some people who liked some of the things I liked: athletics, buying clothes, the same magazines, and because we had a lot in common we would spend ages talking about all the things we liked. I never interrupted them; I waited for them to finish before I spoke. This is because I learnt that if I did interrupt them, they may not want to speak to me again.

I found them interesting and we would often walk home together, still talking. Sometimes we would be invited by the mums into each other's houses for tea and sometimes we would sleep over. We all knew that we had to be polite, say 'please' and 'thank you', not play the music too loud and when we were told it was bedtime we went to bed. Of course, we did not want to, but if we did not do this then the mums might not invite us again.

Some people may not know:

- how to interact with others
- what interests other people have and so cannot strike up a conversation, which can lead to boredom, frustration and isolation.

Some service users may have dementia and may not be able to remember the conversation and follow it, or may be on medication which may affect their sense of reality.

## HOW DIFFERENT PEOPLE INTERACT

Some people say that assertive people get the most friends. I think we individually choose the people we want to spend more time with, which is why we have them as friends. It may take a little longer to get to know a quiet person whereas an assertive person may be a little overpowering. Knowing someone who is a good organizer can be an advantage, but you may not want to have someone else organizing you all the time. Equally, the organized person may not want disorganized friends who need organizing.

Some residents who move into a residential home may find it difficult to get to know where everything is and to get to know everyone. Residents who have been there a long time may have their own little groups of friends and/or acquaintances and may have forgotten how difficult it was for them when they moved in and may not realize that the new resident will need a bit of help in finding out where everything is, what happens in the home and getting to know new people.

Large residential homes can be daunting when the resident first moves in. The resident may forget where their bedroom is or where the dining room is, and this can make the resident choose to stay in his/her room for fear of getting lost and looking stupid.

## Useful tip

Why not have a buddy system where a resident is asked to buddy a new resident? The buddy can show the new resident around, sit with them at mealtimes, explain who does the washing of the clothes and when, introduce the new resident to everyone else. This will give the existing resident a responsibility and they can start planning what they will need to tell the new resident.

Many large residential homes have an activity coordinator and many activities are arranged.

✍ Does anyone review the activities to see if they still meet
the service user's needs?                                            Yes/No

If you have answered 'No', what can you do about it?

. . . . . . . . . . . . . . . . . . . . . . . . . . . . . . . . . . . . . . . . . . . . . . . . . . . . . . . .

. . . . . . . . . . . . . . . . . . . . . . . . . . . . . . . . . . . . . . . . . . . . . . . . . . . . . . . .

. . . . . . . . . . . . . . . . . . . . . . . . . . . . . . . . . . . . . . . . . . . . . . . . . . . . . . . .

✍ Are the quieter perhaps less able residents supported to join in?    Yes/No

If you have answered 'No', what can you do about it?

. . . . . . . . . . . . . . . . . . . . . . . . . . . . . . . . . . . . . . . . . . . . . . .

. . . . . . . . . . . . . . . . . . . . . . . . . . . . . . . . . . . . . . . . . . . . . . .

. . . . . . . . . . . . . . . . . . . . . . . . . . . . . . . . . . . . . . . . . . . . . . .

✍ Are service users who are wheelchair users asked if they want
to join in the activity?                                               Yes/No

If you have answered 'No', what can you do about it?

. . . . . . . . . . . . . . . . . . . . . . . . . . . . . . . . . . . . . . . . . . . . . . .

. . . . . . . . . . . . . . . . . . . . . . . . . . . . . . . . . . . . . . . . . . . . . . .

. . . . . . . . . . . . . . . . . . . . . . . . . . . . . . . . . . . . . . . . . . . . . . .

The way we look and the skills we have or do not have in many situations encourage people either to want to talk to us or to avoid us.

Knowing the service user may help you to think and plan ahead for potential consequences, e.g. if the service user is quiet and/or non-verbal, how can you support him to communicate with others, or if he is loud and outgoing will he overpower people and frighten them off?

A person with Asperger syndrome, a condition associated with impaired social skills, may not say 'Hello' when entering a room, or 'Goodbye' when leaving it. If he feels uncomfortable, he may hijack the conversation and talk about something he feels comfortable with. His condition means that he finds it difficult to see another person's point of view and this can lead to a lot of misunderstanding.

✍ Please tick which terms best describe the service user you support.

| Qualities of the service user | ✓ |
| --- | --- |
| Quiet | |
| Non-verbal | |
| Withdrawn | |
| Assertive, outgoing | |
| Loud | |
| Abrupt | |
| Visually impaired | |

| | |
|---|---|
| Hard of hearing | |
| Overweight | |
| Underweight | |
| Other: | |

✎ Will the description affect people's responses to the service user?  Yes/No

If you have answered 'Yes', please say what you can do about it:

. . . . . . . . . . . . . . . . . . . . . . . . . . . . . . . . . . . . . . . . . . . . . . . . . . . . . . . . .

. . . . . . . . . . . . . . . . . . . . . . . . . . . . . . . . . . . . . . . . . . . . . . . . . . . . . . . . .

. . . . . . . . . . . . . . . . . . . . . . . . . . . . . . . . . . . . . . . . . . . . . . . . . . . . . . . . .

✎ Does the person you support have good social skills?          Yes/No

Think of where you went recently with a service user, e.g. to the shops or library, and ask yourself, did the service user communicate? If so, how (verbal, through body language, smiling etc.)?

. . . . . . . . . . . . . . . . . . . . . . . . . . . . . . . . . . . . . . . . . . . . . . . . . . . . . . . . .

. . . . . . . . . . . . . . . . . . . . . . . . . . . . . . . . . . . . . . . . . . . . . . . . . . . . . . . . .

. . . . . . . . . . . . . . . . . . . . . . . . . . . . . . . . . . . . . . . . . . . . . . . . . . . . . . . . .

Did they politely acknowledge people or was the service user shy and have his head down, looking at the floor and ignoring everyone?

. . . . . . . . . . . . . . . . . . . . . . . . . . . . . . . . . . . . . . . . . . . . . . . . . . . . . . . . .

. . . . . . . . . . . . . . . . . . . . . . . . . . . . . . . . . . . . . . . . . . . . . . . . . . . . . . . . .

. . . . . . . . . . . . . . . . . . . . . . . . . . . . . . . . . . . . . . . . . . . . . . . . . . . . . . . . .

✎ Was the service user too friendly or overpowering to others?     Yes/No

If you answered 'Yes', what can you do about this?

. . . . . . . . . . . . . . . . . . . . . . . . . . . . . . . . . . . . . . . . . . . . . . . . . . . . . . . . .

. . . . . . . . . . . . . . . . . . . . . . . . . . . . . . . . . . . . . . . . . . . . . . . . . . . . . . . . .

. . . . . . . . . . . . . . . . . . . . . . . . . . . . . . . . . . . . . . . . . . . . . . . . . . . . . . . . .

✎ Was there anything else that he did which gives an indication of his level of social skills?

. . . . . . . . . . . . . . . . . . . . . . . . . . . . . . . . . . . . . . . . . . . . . . . . . . . . . . . . .

. . . . . . . . . . . . . . . . . . . . . . . . . . . . . . . . . . . . . . . . . . . . . . . . . . . . . . . . .

. . . . . . . . . . . . . . . . . . . . . . . . . . . . . . . . . . . . . . . . . . . . . . . . . . . . . . . . .

✍ What do you think was the other people's impression of the service user?

. . . . . . . . . . . . . . . . . . . . . . . . . . . . . . . . . . . . . . . . . . . . . . . . . . . . . .

. . . . . . . . . . . . . . . . . . . . . . . . . . . . . . . . . . . . . . . . . . . . . . . . . . . . . .

. . . . . . . . . . . . . . . . . . . . . . . . . . . . . . . . . . . . . . . . . . . . . . . . . . . . . .

---

When you first learnt what a friend was and the value of having a friend, you then:

- learnt to choose who you wanted to be with

- chose who you did not want to be with

- learnt what behaviour was acceptable and what was not acceptable.

---

✍ Has the service user got a choice in who he mixes with and who he wishes to avoid?                                    Yes/No

Please explain your answer:

. . . . . . . . . . . . . . . . . . . . . . . . . . . . . . . . . . . . . . . . . . . . . . . . . . . . . .

. . . . . . . . . . . . . . . . . . . . . . . . . . . . . . . . . . . . . . . . . . . . . . . . . . . . . .

. . . . . . . . . . . . . . . . . . . . . . . . . . . . . . . . . . . . . . . . . . . . . . . . . . . . . .

✍ If the service user needs to learn social skills, he can learn them from a good role model. Are you a good role model?          Yes/No

Please explain your answer.

. . . . . . . . . . . . . . . . . . . . . . . . . . . . . . . . . . . . . . . . . . . . . . . . . . . . . .

. . . . . . . . . . . . . . . . . . . . . . . . . . . . . . . . . . . . . . . . . . . . . . . . . . . . . .

. . . . . . . . . . . . . . . . . . . . . . . . . . . . . . . . . . . . . . . . . . . . . . . . . . . . . .

Some service users may not want or need a friend. At the point in time you ask them, it may be that a service user's needs are instead to watch a bird that comes into the garden every day, the lady who regularly walks past their window, a favourite object or a volunteer to take him out now and again, an advocate who will speak up on his behalf, or someone who he could have written communication with, for example a pen pal or online friend in a chatroom. It is fine if the service user communicates that they do not want friendship at the time you ask them.

# Maintaining Existing Friendships

## SUPPORTING FRIENDSHIPS

Friendships are very important and some service users may need help and support in maintaining their existing friendships.

Service users may experience problems in maintaining friendships for the following reasons:

- People with dementia may not recognize their friends or be able to communicate with them.

- People with a learning disability may not be able to communicate or understand the importance of keeping the arrangements they have made to meet their friends.

- People with a mental health need may not be well on the day to meet the friend or understand the importance of keeping the arrangements they have made to meet their friends.

If the service user needs help, you can help maintain the relationships by providing tools to enable the service user to communicate. Making a family tree, with photographs, will help the service user to remember who is in the family and keep track of it as it grows.

You can also enable the service user to invite their friends or neighbours to their house, though you will need to consider if there are risks attached to doing this, for example:

- stealing from the service user

- abusing the service user

- compromising the safety of the other service users and staff.

Is the house reasonably tidy? If not the friend or neighbour may not want to visit again or may tell others and then the service user gets talked about.

Service users may need help in getting to the place where they wish to go to meet their friends and this can be in the form of:

- applying for a bus pass
- knowing which bus to catch
- needing staff to go with them for confidence
- needing a wheelchair to get around in (if they do not currently have a wheelchair, see the GP for a referral).

✍ If or when service users or staff move from your place of work, does your workplace encourage people to stay in touch?     Yes/No

If you answered 'No', please explain why, and what you could do to enable this to happen. (All too often, people come into a service user's life and, when they leave, that can be the end of a relationship when it could turn into a lasting friendship.)

. . . . . . . . . . . . . . . . . . . . . . . . . . . . . . . . . . . . . . . . . . . . .

. . . . . . . . . . . . . . . . . . . . . . . . . . . . . . . . . . . . . . . . . . . . .

. . . . . . . . . . . . . . . . . . . . . . . . . . . . . . . . . . . . . . . . . . . . .

If not done correctly, some people can feel that they are being forced into a friendship. It needs to be done sensitively. The person's body language (e.g. lack of eye contact, closed body language) will tell you if they do not want to have a friendship with a particular person. Friendships should happen naturally and not be forced.

Some friendships are not straightforward and you will need to check with your manager if there are restrictions under the Mental Health Act or Court Protection Orders that affect the friendship (for more on this, see p.74 and p.90).

Think about the following:

Do you need to be:

- present prior to the service user meeting his friend because the service user is nervous or anxious?
- present during the meeting because the service user is nervous or anxious or needs you to communicate for him?
- present after the meeting in case the service user needs to talk over what happened?

✐ Please tick which type of friendship the service user has.

| Types of friendship | ✓ |
| --- | --- |
| Seeing each other regularly | |
| Not seeing each other regularly | |
| Seeing each other at the day service or college | |
| Seeing each other when staff gives the service user a lift | |
| By telephone | |
| By writing letters | |
| By email | |
| By occasional postcard or Christmas card | |

Please consider the following:

- Is the communication initiated only by the service user?
- Does the friend communicate back?
- Is the friendship initiated only by the friend?
- Are either parties domineering or abusive?

✐ An important question to ask yourself is whether the service user is happy or unhappy with the friendship he has: does he need any additional support?                                     Yes/No

If you have answered 'yes', what help does he need?

. . . . . . . . . . . . . . . . . . . . . . . . . . . . . . . . . . . . . . . . . . . . . . .

. . . . . . . . . . . . . . . . . . . . . . . . . . . . . . . . . . . . . . . . . . . . . . .

. . . . . . . . . . . . . . . . . . . . . . . . . . . . . . . . . . . . . . . . . . . . . . .

Spending time on the Internet or email can be seen by some as a waste of time and a way of escaping. However, being able to use the Internet or email can enable people to connect.

Read the questions below and think about whether any of the answers you give exhibit barriers to a service user maintaining a friendship.

✍ Are the people you support encouraged to talk about their
friends? Yes/No

If you have answered 'No', what are the consequences of this?

. . . . . . . . . . . . . . . . . . . . . . . . . . . . . . . . . . . . . . . . . . . . . . . . . . . . . . . . . .

. . . . . . . . . . . . . . . . . . . . . . . . . . . . . . . . . . . . . . . . . . . . . . . . . . . . . . . . . .

. . . . . . . . . . . . . . . . . . . . . . . . . . . . . . . . . . . . . . . . . . . . . . . . . . . . . . . . . .

✍ If it is a residential setting, does the house encourage the
service users to put up photographs of their family or friends? Yes/No

If you have answered 'No', what can you do about this?

. . . . . . . . . . . . . . . . . . . . . . . . . . . . . . . . . . . . . . . . . . . . . . . . . . . . . . . . . .

. . . . . . . . . . . . . . . . . . . . . . . . . . . . . . . . . . . . . . . . . . . . . . . . . . . . . . . . . .

. . . . . . . . . . . . . . . . . . . . . . . . . . . . . . . . . . . . . . . . . . . . . . . . . . . . . . . . . .

✍ Is the person you support losing contact with a friend who they want to
keep? If so, can you think of why and what could be done about it?

. . . . . . . . . . . . . . . . . . . . . . . . . . . . . . . . . . . . . . . . . . . . . . . . . . . . . . . . . .

. . . . . . . . . . . . . . . . . . . . . . . . . . . . . . . . . . . . . . . . . . . . . . . . . . . . . . . . . .

. . . . . . . . . . . . . . . . . . . . . . . . . . . . . . . . . . . . . . . . . . . . . . . . . . . . . . . . . .

✍ Can the friends of the service user just pop in for a coffee? Yes/No

If you answered 'No', please explain why and what can be done about this:

. . . . . . . . . . . . . . . . . . . . . . . . . . . . . . . . . . . . . . . . . . . . . . . . . . . . . . . . . .

. . . . . . . . . . . . . . . . . . . . . . . . . . . . . . . . . . . . . . . . . . . . . . . . . . . . . . . . . .

. . . . . . . . . . . . . . . . . . . . . . . . . . . . . . . . . . . . . . . . . . . . . . . . . . . . . . . . . .

✍ Does the friend live far away? If so, is there an opportunity
for the service user to have the friend stay over? Yes/No

If you answered 'No', please explain why and what can be done about this:

. . . . . . . . . . . . . . . . . . . . . . . . . . . . . . . . . . . . . . . . . . . . . . . . . . . . . . . . . .

. . . . . . . . . . . . . . . . . . . . . . . . . . . . . . . . . . . . . . . . . . . . . . . . . . . . . . . . . .

. . . . . . . . . . . . . . . . . . . . . . . . . . . . . . . . . . . . . . . . . . . . . . . . . . . . . . . . . .

✍ Can the service user receive and make telephone calls in private?  Yes/No

If you answered 'No', please explain why and what can be done about this:

.............................................................

.............................................................

.............................................................

✍ Does the service user need help to dial the numbers?         Yes/No

Does the service user have the telephone number of his friend or friends in his room, perhaps in an address book or on a notice board in his room?    Yes/No
If you answered 'No' to the above, is the telephone number in the office?
                                                              Yes/No
If you answered 'Yes', why is it in the office?

.............................................................

.............................................................

What can you do about this?

.............................................................

.............................................................

How do you think the service user feels having to ask you for the number all the time?

.............................................................

.............................................................

Can the service user keep in touch by writing a letter and sending it?   Yes/No
Does he need any help with buying the writing pad, envelopes and stamps, or posting them?                                       Yes/No

If you have answered 'yes', what help does he need?

.............................................................

.............................................................

Receiving letters through the post can be very important to some people; it is something to look forward to and if the service user cannot read that does not matter as someone else can read it for him. Remember that the service user should open his own mail, unless he cannot physically do it.

✍ If you work in a residential setting is there a place where the
service user and friend or visitor can go?                    Yes/No

If you answered 'No', what can you do about it?

. . . . . . . . . . . . . . . . . . . . . . . . . . . . . . . . . . . . . . . . . . . . . . . . . . . . . . . .

. . . . . . . . . . . . . . . . . . . . . . . . . . . . . . . . . . . . . . . . . . . . . . . . . . . . . . . .

. . . . . . . . . . . . . . . . . . . . . . . . . . . . . . . . . . . . . . . . . . . . . . . . . . . . . . . .

The risk assessment needs to include many areas, and examples of these
could be:

- assessing the vulnerability of the service user or friend
- considering whether the service user goes out or goes out and stays
  out all night: is he safe?
- assessing the vulnerability of the staff
- assessing the support the service user may need before, during or
  after seeing his friend and what type of support, e.g. can you give
  this support or does it need to be a *trained counsellor*?

**Q:** What happens if a service user has the capacity to make a decision and
chooses to have a vulnerable friendship?

**A:** A risk assessment will need to be put in place and signed by the service
user.

Advice and information will need to be available about keeping oneself safe,
and support should the service user change their mind about the friendship
(more on risk assessments on pp.61–62).

# Supporting the Service User to Establish a New Friendship

If a service user does want to develop a friendship or relationship, whether or not you need to undertake planning will depend on the person you are supporting: whether the development of friendship can be developed independently in a spontaneous way, or will require assistance. You should discuss with the service user the level of support he requires and from whom, e.g. you, a staff member of the same gender and/or culture, or a family member etc.

Depending on where you work, your policies and procedures may say that you will need to arrange a time to discuss the planning with your manager as well. Your manager may advise you to make a start before you meet with the service user: this could be to look at what the person's interests are.

## WHERE WE FIND FRIENDS

There will be times when we all want or need new friends. This could be because we are new to an area, have breakdowns in previous friendships due to divorce, or outgrow our friends as our interests change and we develop. But how do you support a service user in their decision to seek out a new friendship or relationship?

Some places to find people who may become a friend include:

- social venues where people chat – pubs, bars
- joining a group or club of people who are like-minded or who share the same interests
- online social networking sites
- work
- college.

A tip for staff: if a past or current service user finds you on a social networking site you should not accept their invitation to add you as their friend. You have a paid professional relationship with the service user; your private life is your private boundary. If you add a service user you are crossing the boundaries of professionalism. This could also cause confusion of boundaries to the service user.

As a social care worker, you must uphold public trust and confidence in social care services.

In particular you must not:

**5.4** Form inappropriate personal relationships with service users;

**5.8** Behave in a way, in work or outside work, which would call into question your suitability to work in social care services. (GSCC Code of Practice standard 5)

Special Friends Online is a great website for people with a learning disability, their carers, family and volunteers to meet people, make friends and talk to people online. Visit www.specialfriendsonline.com for more information.

✍ If you want a friend for yourself, where do you go to look for one?

. . . . . . . . . . . . . . . . . . . . . . . . . . . . . . . . . . . . . . . . . . . . . . . .

. . . . . . . . . . . . . . . . . . . . . . . . . . . . . . . . . . . . . . . . . . . . . . . .

. . . . . . . . . . . . . . . . . . . . . . . . . . . . . . . . . . . . . . . . . . . . . . . .

It is important to avoid assuming that the pub is a good place to meet new friends. Of course, you can make friends in a pub, but is it the right environment? What will the people in there and the service user have in common?

Here are some ideas for venues or interests that a service user could pursue as an alternative; arrange a time with the service user to go through them. Use photographs or pictures to show the service user if the activities below will be unfamiliar to them. Depending on the individual it may be better for him to see one picture or photo at a time and watch his response, rather than show them all at once as this could be confusing.

✍ Tick the activities the service user is interested in and add any others that interest them:

| Activities at sports centre | ✓ |
|---|---|
| • tai chi | |
| • yoga | |
| • swimming | |
| • badminton | |
| • table tennis | |
| • football | |
| • rugby | |
| • netball | |
| • pool | |
| • snooker | |
| • darts | |
| • other | |
| Artistic activities: would the service user like to learn to paint, draw, help out with back stage at theatre groups perhaps? | |
| Healthy activities: does he enjoy walking or keeping fit? Would he like to be part of a walking group or help someone to walk their dog? | |
| Studying: would he like to learn to read or write? Why not join a college course? | ✓ |
| Church or other religious activity? | |
| Reading or looking at books, joining the library, or reading book clubs | |
| Taking or looking at photographs: would he like to join a photography group? | |
| Creative activities like pottery or other handicrafts | |
| Relaxation groups | |
| Inviting people round to watch a video or DVD: find out what films the service user really likes | |
| Taking a holiday (without staff). There are various organizations that cater for the single person, either with or without a disability | |
| Accessing a computer: perhaps complete a computer course or invite people round to look at the brilliant things the service user does on his computer | |
| Gardening or growing vegetables: perhaps look into having a small vegetable patch in the garden or an allotment | |
| Local history and points of interest: find out about historic talks on the area | |
| Learing to ride a bike, or hiring a bike to go out cycling | |

There are many large residential homes across the UK and no doubt many service users may wish to meet other people, whether it is for friendship or something more. Managers can accommodate this by liaising with other homes' managers and arranging for some service users to visit their home and vice versa if this is what the service user would like to do.

✍ Feel free to add your own suggestions to the list, and remember that it could be either watching or doing these activities.

. . . . . . . . . . . . . . . . . . . . . . . . . . . . . . . . . . . . . . . . . . . . . . . . .

. . . . . . . . . . . . . . . . . . . . . . . . . . . . . . . . . . . . . . . . . . . . . . . . .

. . . . . . . . . . . . . . . . . . . . . . . . . . . . . . . . . . . . . . . . . . . . . . . . .

Once you have identified an interest, think about how to organize it. Encourage the service user to look at their weekly events: they may have a busy week and only have a Tuesday free to go out.

## HOW DO WE CHOOSE NEW FRIENDS?

Do you choose your friends by:

- looks
- age
- personality
- gender
- having the same interests
- having different interests?

✍ If you asked a service user what a friend was, would he know?     Yes/No

Can the service user tell you what type of person he would like
to have as a friend?                                                Yes/No

Can the service user tell you how many friends he would like?       Yes/No

. . . . . . . . . . . . . . . . . . . . . . . . . . . . . . . . . . . . . . . . . . . . . . . . .

. . . . . . . . . . . . . . . . . . . . . . . . . . . . . . . . . . . . . . . . . . . . . . . . .

. . . . . . . . . . . . . . . . . . . . . . . . . . . . . . . . . . . . . . . . . . . . . . . . .

*Remember:* regardless of the person's ability, everyone can communicate with who they like. For people who have difficulties communicating, you will be able to see service users' facial expression or body language change when you show them photographs or when they see someone they like: this may even be simply blinking an eyelid.

In some cases you can work with service users to ascertain what they want, for example an older person may want a friend of a similar age to reminisce with; a younger person with mental health difficulties may say they want a friend for self-support around similar feelings or emotions; a person with learning disabilities may not be able to express what he wants or needs but his family may also like to have input.

## PROVIDING OPPORTUNITIES TO SOCIALIZE

If the people you support do not have opportunities to meet people, the likelihood of meeting others and making friends is going to be very limited.

**12.3**: service users interests are recorded and they are given opportunities for stimulation through leisure and recreational activities in and outside the home which suit their needs, preferences and capacities; particular consideration is given to people with dementia and other cognitive impairments, those with visual, hearing or dual sensory impairments, those with physical disabilities or learning disabilities. (Care Home for Older People Standard 12)

If the service user does not talk to people, he will not make any friends.

✍ What does 'opportunities to socialize' mean to you?

. . . . . . . . . . . . . . . . . . . . . . . . . . . . . . . . . . . . . . . . . . . . . . . . . . . .

. . . . . . . . . . . . . . . . . . . . . . . . . . . . . . . . . . . . . . . . . . . . . . . . . . . .

. . . . . . . . . . . . . . . . . . . . . . . . . . . . . . . . . . . . . . . . . . . . . . . . . . . .

I guess your answer included one or both of these: to meet people I know, to meet new people who have the same or similar interests as me.

✍ Are there opportunities for the people you support to be with people who:

| | |
|---|---|
| Have the same or similar interests? | Yes/No |
| Are not paid staff from the home or at day centre/workshop? | Yes/No |

If there are not any opportunities, what can you do about this?

. . . . . . . . . . . . . . . . . . . . . . . . . . . . . . . . . . . . . . . . . . . . . . . . . . . .

. . . . . . . . . . . . . . . . . . . . . . . . . . . . . . . . . . . . . . . . . . . . . . . . . . . .

. . . . . . . . . . . . . . . . . . . . . . . . . . . . . . . . . . . . . . . . . . . . . . . . . . . .

## Activities

✍ How often during the week (including the weekend) do you go out socializing, including popping round to friends for a drink or meal?

. . . . . . . . . . . . . . . . . . . . . . . . . . . . . . . . . . . . . . . . . . .

. . . . . . . . . . . . . . . . . . . . . . . . . . . . . . . . . . . . . . . . . . .

. . . . . . . . . . . . . . . . . . . . . . . . . . . . . . . . . . . . . . . . . . .

✍ 1. What feelings do you have, for example, nervous or excited, before you go out?

. . . . . . . . . . . . . . . . . . . . . . . . . . . . . . . . . . . . . . . . . . .

2. How about while you are out?

. . . . . . . . . . . . . . . . . . . . . . . . . . . . . . . . . . . . . . . . . . .

3. And when you return back home?

. . . . . . . . . . . . . . . . . . . . . . . . . . . . . . . . . . . . . . . . . . .

✍ Now put yourself in the position of the service user and ask the same questions:

1. . . . . . . . . . . . . . . . . . . . . . . . . . . . . . . . . . . . . . . . . . .

2. . . . . . . . . . . . . . . . . . . . . . . . . . . . . . . . . . . . . . . . . . .

3. . . . . . . . . . . . . . . . . . . . . . . . . . . . . . . . . . . . . . . . . . .

If the people you support do not have opportunities to go out, they will not experience all the different feelings and emotions that going out can bring.

## Social opportunities

| Social opportunity | Over a period of four weeks how often do you: | Over a period of four weeks how often does the service user: |
|---|---|---|
| Invite a friend round for a meal | | |
| Write a letter to a friend, with or without help | | |
| Make or receive a telephone call from a friend | | |

| | | |
|---|---|---|
| Send or receive a text or an email from a friend | | |
| Go to a disco or night club | | |
| Go to the pub | | |
| Go to keep fit, gym, aerobics, leisure club, etc. | | |
| Participate as a member of a group | | |
| Other | | |

✍ Now you have completed the chart, what does it tell you?

. . . . . . . . . . . . . . . . . . . . . . . . . . . . . . . . . . . . . . . . . . . . . . . . . . . .

. . . . . . . . . . . . . . . . . . . . . . . . . . . . . . . . . . . . . . . . . . . . . . . . . . . .

. . . . . . . . . . . . . . . . . . . . . . . . . . . . . . . . . . . . . . . . . . . . . . . . . . . .

✍ Do your answers relate to lack of opportunities?          Yes/No

If you answered 'Yes', what can you do about it?

. . . . . . . . . . . . . . . . . . . . . . . . . . . . . . . . . . . . . . . . . . . . . . . . . . . .

. . . . . . . . . . . . . . . . . . . . . . . . . . . . . . . . . . . . . . . . . . . . . . . . . . . .

. . . . . . . . . . . . . . . . . . . . . . . . . . . . . . . . . . . . . . . . . . . . . . . . . . . .

## SERVICE USERS WHO CHOOSE NOT TO SOCIALIZE

There are service users who are not going out with people outside of their home, nor are they socializing with whom they live with: there can be many reasons for this. They may be quiet people and it is the confident and assertive service users who get the attention of staff where they can say they would like to go out somewhere or are asked if they would like to go out. Alternatively, some service users may prefer to attend the activities on offer within the home.

It is important to support service users no matter how quiet or shy they are, as they may be experiencing feelings of loneliness or isolation.

# Supporting the Service User's Self-Esteem and Feelings

Self-image is how you see yourself. If you do not feel good about yourself and have poor self-esteem, you provide others with a negative image in how you behave and communicate. If you give out this negative impression, it is more likely that you will receive a negative response. People may think that you are incompetent or unfriendly, and may choose to ignore or avoid you, which can have the effect of reinforcing feelings of low self-esteem.

If you receive negative messages from people often, you eventually believe them yourself.

✎ Do you think that any of the service users show signs of poor self-image? Please explain your answer:

. . . . . . . . . . . . . . . . . . . . . . . . . . . . . . . . . . . . . . . . . . . . . . . . . . .
. . . . . . . . . . . . . . . . . . . . . . . . . . . . . . . . . . . . . . . . . . . . . . . . . . .

What could you do about it?

. . . . . . . . . . . . . . . . . . . . . . . . . . . . . . . . . . . . . . . . . . . . . . . . . . .
. . . . . . . . . . . . . . . . . . . . . . . . . . . . . . . . . . . . . . . . . . . . . . . . . . .
. . . . . . . . . . . . . . . . . . . . . . . . . . . . . . . . . . . . . . . . . . . . . . . . . . .
. . . . . . . . . . . . . . . . . . . . . . . . . . . . . . . . . . . . . . . . . . . . . . . . . . .

Feeling good can raise confidence and self-esteem: I can feel good just by looking forward to going out and meeting up with friends, or because of the clothes I am wearing, my perfume or my make-up, or after a workout at the gym.

For some people, wearing their favourite clothes can enable them to feel confident and secure and the people you support should be able to choose what to wear. Some may need a little help in choosing appropriate clothes for the occasion or the weather.

When visiting a home for older people recently, a resident looked well and happy and excitedly told me that a carer had put her make-up on for her and varnished her nails. She then whispered to me that a different carer last week put some cream on her chin to get rid of the facial hair and finished by saying that she felt 'like a million dollars!' These tasks were something the service user always did for herself but can no longer do.

✍ What makes you feel good and raises your confidence and self-esteem?

. . . . . . . . . . . . . . . . . . . . . . . . . . . . . . . . . . . . . . . . . . . . . . . . . . . . . . .

. . . . . . . . . . . . . . . . . . . . . . . . . . . . . . . . . . . . . . . . . . . . . . . . . . . . . . .

. . . . . . . . . . . . . . . . . . . . . . . . . . . . . . . . . . . . . . . . . . . . . . . . . . . . . . .

Do you know what makes the person you support feel good and raises his confidence and self-esteem? What is it?

. . . . . . . . . . . . . . . . . . . . . . . . . . . . . . . . . . . . . . . . . . . . . . . . . . . . . . .

. . . . . . . . . . . . . . . . . . . . . . . . . . . . . . . . . . . . . . . . . . . . . . . . . . . . . . .

. . . . . . . . . . . . . . . . . . . . . . . . . . . . . . . . . . . . . . . . . . . . . . . . . . . . . . .

Examples of how confidence and self-esteem can be decreased include being in company of people who:

- say negative things about you
- are always moaning
- are always talking about you and not to you.

✍ Can you think of any more?

. . . . . . . . . . . . . . . . . . . . . . . . . . . . . . . . . . . . . . . . . . . . . . . . . . . . . . .

. . . . . . . . . . . . . . . . . . . . . . . . . . . . . . . . . . . . . . . . . . . . . . . . . . . . . . .

. . . . . . . . . . . . . . . . . . . . . . . . . . . . . . . . . . . . . . . . . . . . . . . . . . . . . . .

## SUPPORTING SELF-ESTEEM WHEN MAKING FRIENDSHIPS

When you go out with a service user, both you and the service user are on view, and may be judged or viewed with curiosity by those who see you. Why is this? This is because not everyone is accepted and integrated into the community, and adults who live in residential care homes or who have domiciliary support can be marginalized. As social care staff you still have a long way to go to enable many service users to be accepted.

Take some time now to think of the preparation work you and the service user need to do before going outside the front door, and once you are outside of the door, then the next steps to follow the planned action through.

1. . . . . . . . . . . . . . . . . . . . . . . . . . . . . . . . . . . . . . . . . . . . . . . . . . . . . . . .

. . . . . . . . . . . . . . . . . . . . . . . . . . . . . . . . . . . . . . . . . . . . . . . . . . . . . . . .

2. . . . . . . . . . . . . . . . . . . . . . . . . . . . . . . . . . . . . . . . . . . . . . . . . . . . . . . .

. . . . . . . . . . . . . . . . . . . . . . . . . . . . . . . . . . . . . . . . . . . . . . . . . . . . . . . .

3. . . . . . . . . . . . . . . . . . . . . . . . . . . . . . . . . . . . . . . . . . . . . . . . . . . . . . . .

. . . . . . . . . . . . . . . . . . . . . . . . . . . . . . . . . . . . . . . . . . . . . . . . . . . . . . . .

4. . . . . . . . . . . . . . . . . . . . . . . . . . . . . . . . . . . . . . . . . . . . . . . . . . . . . . . .

. . . . . . . . . . . . . . . . . . . . . . . . . . . . . . . . . . . . . . . . . . . . . . . . . . . . . . . .

Did your answers cover any of the following for you both?

- Appropriate clothing for the activity (e.g. if you are going line dancing what would you wear?)
- Appropriate clothing for the weather (e.g. in hot sunshine would one wear a heavy coat?)
- Clothes that fit properly and are not too bright as this can attract the 'wrong' kind of attention
- Clean clothes, hair, shoes, glasses and face
- If the service user is a wheelchair user, a clean chair which is in good working order.

Also, think about your journey once you have left the property. Think about how you walk with the service user: side by side is fine, but holding hands will make the service user stand out. Will you communicate to the service user or with the service user? If so, how? Do you know how to get the chair up and down the kerb safely?

If you are going out in the car, will the service user sit in the front or the back? Unless the service user prefers to sit in the back or the risk assessment says the service user should sit in the back, then they have every right to sit in the front. To be sitting in the back when two staff are in the front or the front passenger seat is empty could show the public that the service user is second best and something is 'wrong' with the service user. This may also have the effect of reducing the service user's sense of self-esteem.

I visited a residential service when a staff member was supporting a person with a learning disability to go to the shops. When the staff member asked if everyone was ready I had to advise her discreetly that she should not go out yet as she had a wet stain on her own white top. Although this was clearly visible, the staff member said, 'It is OK, let's go!' I pointed out to her that walking around with a noticeable stain would draw attention and give a poor impression. She insisted it didn't matter, it was only tea. Luckily, I was able to explain why it was worth waiting until it was clean and dry, and she did wait.

When discussing it with the staff member, it became apparent that she was so conscientious about meeting the service user's own needs and not wishing to let her down, that she did not consider the impression she would give to the people she met and how this reflects on the service user and the organization she works for.

## DEALING WITH LONELINESS

Isolation and limited contact can happen anywhere, at home, in small or large group homes. This can be due to a number of reasons.

- In some residential homes all the service users live together, go to the same day centre or college and/or go on holiday together, but the quieter or shy residents in the home may not be supported and encouraged to interact with other service users who live there. It is sometimes thought by staff that friends are not important or needed in a service user's life.

- There may not be enough staff in a residential setting to go out with the service user, so they may only go out now and again.

- The service user may exhibit behaviour that could upset others, or there may be limited destinations to visit nearby.

- Staff may not have the knowledge to support service users to build or rebuild social skills and have social opportunities.

- A service user may be too unwell to go out without support.

- A service user may be self-conscious of their physical appearance – perhaps because they have had a stroke, or wear a catheter with a bag strapped to their leg, or experience incontinence and are reluctant to travel far from a toilet.

- Service users may live by themselves in a small area where everyone keeps themselves to themselves.

✍ Think about whether you have seen any of the above happening in your workplace.

. . . . . . . . . . . . . . . . . . . . . . . . . . . . . . . . . . . . . . . . . . . . . . . . . . .

. . . . . . . . . . . . . . . . . . . . . . . . . . . . . . . . . . . . . . . . . . . . . . . . . . .

. . . . . . . . . . . . . . . . . . . . . . . . . . . . . . . . . . . . . . . . . . . . . . . . . . .

There are always ways to help to limit isolation and loneliness.

If the service user is shy, provide them with tactful support. The service user could start by talking to the person he sits next to on the bus or the person at the video shop perhaps, or start getting used to the idea of small talk by practising with staff. Start a conversation on something you have in common; what do you think of this weather? Suggest conversational tips, like how to start conversation by giving a compliment to another person.

Some service users will be bed-bound and may only see staff who pop in to feed them and every two hours to turn the service user, etc. This can be very lonely and isolating for the service user.

Here are a few suggestions on how to make them feel less lonely:

- sit with the service user and have a chat
- sit with the service user and look through photographs
- take the company to the service user, e.g. small group of residents in the service user's bedroom having a cup of tea or a 'picnic'.

**12.3**: service users' interests are recorded and they are given opportunities for stimulation through leisure and recreational activities in and outside the home which suit their needs, preferences and capacities; particular consideration is given to people with dementia and other cognitive impairments, those with visual, hearing or dual sensory impairments, those with physical disabilities or learning disabilities. (Care Home for Older People Standard 12)

✍ Can you think of a few more suggestions to reduce isolation and loneliness?:

. . . . . . . . . . . . . . . . . . . . . . . . . . . . . . . . . . . . . . . . . . . . . . . . . . .

. . . . . . . . . . . . . . . . . . . . . . . . . . . . . . . . . . . . . . . . . . . . . . . . . . .

. . . . . . . . . . . . . . . . . . . . . . . . . . . . . . . . . . . . . . . . . . . . . . . . . . .

## Working in the community

If you are going into a person's home, the length of time and the task you are to carry out is very specific and you will not have the opportunity to stay for long periods and chat with the resident. Years ago neighbours would pop into each other's house for a cup of tea but that does not seem to happen so much these days.

Sometimes you may be the only person the service user sees and talks to each day. If this is the case and the service user is very lonely, you may wish to discuss this with your manager who may recommend suggesting different activities such as dinner clubs or contacting family.

## Befriending services

Age Concern run a befriending service for older people and there are befriending services for people who have learning disabilities, physical disabilities and mental health needs.

## Holidays

There may be service users who would like to go on holiday but for various reasons cannot go or only have the opportunity to go with the people they live with. There are a variety of holiday companies that provide holidays for the person who wishes to holiday alone. These are holidays for people without disabilities and many can be found on the Internet. You will need to discuss with the service user and others the risks that could be attached to the service user holidaying alone, without staff support. If the service user needs a carer to go on holiday with him then he will need to check with the individual holiday company if a carer can go along as this can be interpreted as the service user not being a single traveller.

There are specific holidays for people with learning and/or physical disabilities which have trained staff to support the service user and these also can be found on the Internet. Holidays that are available include holidays for the single person, both non-disabled and disabled. Some organizations even provide their own carers and some can provide nursing and care services both in the UK and abroad. Others cater for deaf and blind visitors, have level access to dining room and will cater for special diets. It may also be possible to find those that accept guide dogs. For a list of charities and private firms that provide holidays for people with special needs, contact CareLine: www.careline.org.uk/section.asp?docid=267

# The Practicalities of Going Out

## APPREHENSION ABOUT GOING OUT

There may be times when you feel apprehensive about going out with one of the people you support. Equally, the service user may be apprehensive about going out in general and/or going out with you. For instance it may be that in the past the service user did not understand what you meant when you asked him if he wanted to go for a swim. A swim can mean many things, such as swim in a swimming pool or swim in the sea. Some may not know what the word 'swim' means. How did you ask the service user? Did you ask him verbally and he said 'Yes'? Some service users will say 'Yes' to everything as they assume that is what you want to hear.

## FLIGHT OR FIGHT REACTIONS

When we are unsure about something or something frightens us, the 'fight or flight' reaction comes in to play and we have a choice of running away (flight) or staying and facing the situation (fighting).

This is relevant to us all: often we choose to walk away from something that is frightening. We can do this quietly and say 'I do not like this, I need to go' and then leave, or we can do it more demonstratively, by running away and showing signs of fear. Many supported people can say 'I don't like this, I need to go.' However, there are also many that are unable to say this and may leave the area demonstrating behaviour that is not positive (challenging behaviour). It is unfortunate that the service user expresses themselves this way, but it is usually done for a reason which may not immediately be obvious, because the service users are not able to express themselves in another way. If you experience problems with challenging behaviour, you may find the workbook *Supporting Positive Behaviour* very useful.

## PLANNING THE ACTIVITY

**Q:** What can you do to ensure the service user likes the activity he is going to do?

**A**: If the service user has not had the opportunity to go out often, or has not tried any of the activities, then you could try the following.

Once the service user has chosen an activity, break it down into small steps. If the service user wishes to go to line dancing, try the following stages.

1. Book it in the house diary and on the service user's calendar. If he has not got one then perhaps you could ask him if he would like one. If he is unable to acknowledge the purpose of a calendar then you can highlight with a highlighting pen on the calendar when he will be going to line dancing again and put a small picture or photograph of the venue or something that relates to line dancing next to that date. Everyone can then point out to him periodically that this is when he will be going. The morning staff could help him cross off each day leading up to it.

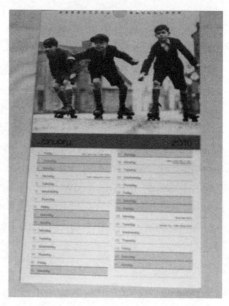

*Visual planning*

2. Arrange to go to the venue before the day of the activity so the service user can see where he is going and it will be more familiar for when he goes the next time. Whichever form of transport you use, keep using it for each occasion for the consistency. Once the service user gains confidence the form of transport can be changed if the service user agrees to this.

3. Ask now and again if he is OK, something brief like 'Are you OK?' Do not overload with words as this can cause distress with some service users.

4. Then go for a coffee or cup of tea, ask the service user how he feels, i.e. happy or sad, and if he would like to go again next week.

5. Go back and write up in the active support care plan what you have learnt and write it in the diary and on the service user's calendar for the next time.

Alternatively, you could arrange to go by car, bus or foot to the venue so the service user can watch one session of line dancing. As before, ask now and again if he is OK and then go to a café. When having a coffee or cup of tea, ask the service user how he feels and ask if he would like to try doing the actual dancing either now or next week. As with the steps above, you should go back and write it up in the active support care plan and write it in the diary and on the service user's calendar for the next time.

Breaking the task down into easily manageable steps will prevent the service user becoming distressed and will give him time to acknowledge what the activity is. There is no pressure put on to him, so that he should feel happy and will want to do it again, possibly with you.

If he does not want to do this one again, make you sure you make this clear on his activity sheet and next time, try the next activity on the list. Be prepared to stop the activity and return home at any point. If we remember horrible things that have happened or if we are forced to do them, we will not want to do them again.

Libraries have a wealth of information on what is happening locally on their notice boards. Why not pop along with the service user and pick up some information?

You will also need to consider the following:

- Will a staff member be needed on the actual day of the activity to support the service user? Can the service user go by themselves, or do they need to be dropped off and picked up? This will be written in detail on the risk assessment.

- If staff are needed to go with the service user, who is the best staff member to go with him? If it is an all-male group session then a male staff member would be better supporting the service user than a female staff member.

- Does it need to be a staff member who takes the service user? Would the service user like a member of the family or a volunteer to support him?

- Finances: who will pay for what?

- Which is the best time of the day or evening to go?

- Are there any concerns you need to be aware of?

You may like to start thinking about what you will do when you are at the service user's chosen venue. Think along the lines of: where, what, how and why?

## WHAT TO DO WHEN YOU ARE GOING OUT

Going anywhere can enable people to build friendships; however, it does depend on how you facilitate this and enable this to happen, and over the next few pages you will read some examples and suggestions.

When you and the service user are going out:

- Dress appropriately.

- Be polite, smile and maintain good eye contact.

- If someone stops to talk to you, include the service user in the conversation.

- Be observant: if the person you are supporting has not been taught social skills, you need to be close to the person and be ready to help if he needs you to. If he gets scared and hits out, you should be close enough to block his arm from hitting the person or you can try to defuse the situation by suggesting doing something else.

### Pub scenario

Here is an example of a social outing for you to read.

✍  A service user fancies a drink and chooses to go to the pub. You are supporting him. The service user has limited finances and is on medication. He has a beer and you have a lemonade. He drinks his drink quickly, and you still have a full glass of lemonade.

What do you think is likely to happen next?

. . . . . . . . . . . . . . . . . . . . . . . . . . . . . . . . . . . . . . . . . . . . . . . .

. . . . . . . . . . . . . . . . . . . . . . . . . . . . . . . . . . . . . . . . . . . . . . . .

. . . . . . . . . . . . . . . . . . . . . . . . . . . . . . . . . . . . . . . . . . . . . . . .

Did your answers cover any of the following?

- The service user may want another drink and may drink that one quickly too.

- He may run out of money.

- His drink may affect his medication.

- He may get drunk.

- The people in the pub think you are mean as you have a drink and the service user does not.

- You may not feel comfortable supporting him and the service user will pick this up and this could make him nervous.
- You may feel that you have to drink your drink quickly.

If you say to the service user, 'You're going to the pub for a drink,' some service users will believe that this is all they are going for and therefore may drink it down in one and will then sit there without a drink.

If you are in the pub, sit so the service user can see others and vice versa. However, if you are sitting at a table this does not really provide good social interaction; standing would be better, but could be tiring, and depending how many are in the pub, could be crowded.

## Line dancing scenario

If the service user has not done line dancing before, a beginner's class would be a good idea. It could also be a good idea for you to join in too, so you can quickly help if the person gets into difficulty. Any kind of dancing is fun; it should soothe the nerves and it is interactive.

## Local walking group

If the service user is not usually active, a few weeks before joining this group, accompany the service user on a few short walks, even if it is only to the shop and back, and increase the distance a little each time.

Has the service user got:

- good walking shoes or trainers?
- socks that don't cause blisters when in contact with the shoes?

Join the service user on the planned walks and, when you introduce yourself to others, give the service user the opportunity to say who he is. Ensure the service user is included in the conversations. This may not be possible all the time; it will depend on the person and how interactive they wish to be. Sometimes too much interaction can be stressful, especially if you like to walk and have some quiet thinking time.

Any activity relieves stress and, depending on the activity, you could lose some weight and feel healthier: it makes you feel good afterwards.

## Interaction

The service user may have limited communication skills. You can still have a conversation with the people you support, for example, if you are sitting in a café or on a bus or train and the person you support is non-verbal, why not take along some magazines or small photo albums or anything to engage in conversation? You do not need to talk non-stop as this could cause anxiety to the service user. Try talking little and often. If the service user does not have any verbal skills he can communicate with a smile or a wink, but do remember that we all like a bit of peace and quiet now and again.

To sit next to a service user with no communication taking place between yourselves can give the impression to potential friends that you are not approachable; if you're not communicating with the service user, why should they?

## MEETING SOMEONE FOR THE FIRST TIME

✍ Take a minute now to think about what you do when you meet someone or join a group for the first time. Write your answer here:

. . . . . . . . . . . . . . . . . . . . . . . . . . . . . . . . . . . . . . . . . . . . . . . . . . . .

. . . . . . . . . . . . . . . . . . . . . . . . . . . . . . . . . . . . . . . . . . . . . . . . . . . .

. . . . . . . . . . . . . . . . . . . . . . . . . . . . . . . . . . . . . . . . . . . . . . . . . . . .

✍ How do you feel when you meet someone or join a group for the first time?

. . . . . . . . . . . . . . . . . . . . . . . . . . . . . . . . . . . . . . . . . . . . . . . . . . . .

. . . . . . . . . . . . . . . . . . . . . . . . . . . . . . . . . . . . . . . . . . . . . . . . . . . .

. . . . . . . . . . . . . . . . . . . . . . . . . . . . . . . . . . . . . . . . . . . . . . . . . . . .

✍ What do you think it would feel like for the service user to meet someone or join a group for the first time?

Excited? Don't know what to expect? Shy? Nervous?

. . . . . . . . . . . . . . . . . . . . . . . . . . . . . . . . . . . . . . . . . . . . . . . . . . . .

. . . . . . . . . . . . . . . . . . . . . . . . . . . . . . . . . . . . . . . . . . . . . . . . . . . .

. . . . . . . . . . . . . . . . . . . . . . . . . . . . . . . . . . . . . . . . . . . . . . . . . . . .

Don't forget to provide practical and emotional support; we all need it at times!

## SELF-DISCLOSURE

We all have a history, including the people you support. For some service users who can communicate, they may self-disclose when meeting someone and tell them about their past. Telling people who we do not know our history can sometimes put them off. If a service user self-harms and tells a person the first time they meet, it is usually an inappropriate level of intimacy according to usual social rules, and can put the other person off. There is a time and place to tell people about your past but usually not until you get to know that person and you can trust them.

However, sometimes self-disclosure is appropriate. If a service user has Tourette's, for example, and shares this with the new person, then this is the person's choice and he may be sharing this in order to explain why he may swear from time to time.

Some people you support may have an interesting history and some new people could be put off by this. Therefore, you may need to discuss with the service user which parts of their history they wish to share with others, and when it would be appropriate to do this. For some people you will need to do the introductions. Please check this with your manager and read your policy on confidentiality about how much information you should give out.

## COMMUNICATING THAT THE SERVICE USER LIKES SOMEONE

If during the activity the service user either shows through body language or expresses verbally that he likes a particular person, then you need to consider several things:

- Is there any risk to the service user or the person that he likes?
- Does the other person feel the same?
- What will the impact be for the service user if the other person does not feel the same?
- Do you need to do something right now, e.g. chat to the person the service user likes, or help the service user give the other person his phone number or arrange to meet here again?

## AT THE END OF A SOCIAL ACTIVITY

## Scenario

**Q**: The service user is just about to finish the first session of the line dancing. Do you both just walk away or do you do the courteous thing of saying how much you have both enjoyed it and hope to be back next time?

**A**: I would do the latter: it's a start and the others will feel good that you both want to join them again.

## REFLECTING

*Discussing the event with the service user*

Away from the group, perhaps on the way home, or at the service user's home, ensure you give the service user the opportunity to talk about how he felt and if he wants to go again. If it is a weekly event, then you really need to ensure that the service user is able to go the following week, and the weeks after that. It is good to have continuity so you may wish to ask your manager if you can go each time with the service user, and ensure that the house diary and the service user's calendar are timetabled to reflect this. Of course, if you feel another staff member could support him better, then you need to tell your manager this.

You also need to reflect back on the event with the service user; what things worked well, what did not work well and what, if anything, you would need to do differently next time. Where possible discuss this with the service user, inform him that you would like to write it in his active support care plan and ask him if this is OK.

# Friendship and Professional Boundaries

Something that service users and staff can find confusing is the difference between personal and professional friendship. Staff have a paid professional relationship with service users, which is very different from a personal friendship. This means that staff are friendly to service users, but be aware of the following:

- Staff are paid to support service users and have a duty to care; they must follow the company's policies and procedures.

- These will clearly outline the roles and responsibilities of staff and by doing this set out boundaries for staff to work within.

- If you do not follow these guidelines, you could leave yourself open to allegations of professional misconduct.

As a social care worker, you must uphold public trust and confidence in social care services. In particular you must not:

**5.4:** Form inappropriate personal relationships with service users. (GSCC Code of Practice 5)

The boundaries provide a standardized approach and provide the service users with the safety to confide in the staff. Here are some examples of boundaries:

- Staff cannot be friends of service users as conflicts of interest may arise.

- Staff are not allowed to keep secrets in the way that friends can keep secrets.

- Staff are not allowed to lend or borrow money to/from a service user as you might with a friend.

- Staff must not have a sexual relationship with a service user.

- If a member of staff has a personal problem, they cannot share it with the service user.

- Staff must not touch service users in an inappropriate way.
- Staff may need to record a lot of information on the service user (for consistency, to share information with others when appropriate, to protect and to meet legislation requirements).

✍ How do you think the service user feels about professional boundaries?

. . . . . . . . . . . . . . . . . . . . . . . . . . . . . . . . . . . . . . . . . . . . . . . . . . . . . . . . . . .

. . . . . . . . . . . . . . . . . . . . . . . . . . . . . . . . . . . . . . . . . . . . . . . . . . . . . . . . . . .

✍ How do you think the service user feels having things written about him?

. . . . . . . . . . . . . . . . . . . . . . . . . . . . . . . . . . . . . . . . . . . . . . . . . . . . . . . . . . .

. . . . . . . . . . . . . . . . . . . . . . . . . . . . . . . . . . . . . . . . . . . . . . . . . . . . . . . . . . .

Imagine how you would feel if a friend recorded everything that you were doing.

One main difference between a friend and a support worker or carer is that the worker has to record things, a friend does not. List two more differences.

✍

1. . . . . . . . . . . . . . . . . . . . . . . . . . . . . . . . . . . . . . . . . . . . . . . . . . . . . . . . . . .

2. . . . . . . . . . . . . . . . . . . . . . . . . . . . . . . . . . . . . . . . . . . . . . . . . . . . . . . . . . .

All staff must make sure that their professional relationships with service users remain of a professional nature at all times, both inside and outside of the workplace.

# Monitoring, Recording, Reporting and Risk

When you are organizing any kind of activity, or observing service users at home, you should be aware of the need to monitor and evaluate the service user carrying out the activity. It will depend on the individual service user as to if and how much you will need to monitor and evaluate what the service user does.

## MONITORING ACTIVITIES

If you have organized an activity, you may need to review the activity after each occasion to begin with and then at set intervals; this will enable you and others to see if the activity is going well; can the level of support be reduced? If the activity is not going well, how can it be adjusted or does the service user want to change the activity? Remember, we change our minds about the activities we choose and the people you support can do this too.

Although it does not sound nice to have to monitor and evaluate aspects of the service user's life, you do have a duty to care and need to ensure that the service user is not being taken advantage of. There is more information on personal and professional boundaries on p.59–60. Where possible, involve the service user and allow them input in the monitoring and evaluation.

## RISK

There are always risks attached to everything we do and risks are not just specific to the people you support. Before we go out, we often think about risks: how we will get there and back safely, will there be people there we know, if not, what will we do, are we meeting a friend first, have we got enough money, what happens if someone approaches us that we do not like, how will we handle it, and so on.

If we are going on a date for the first time, there will also be these potential risks and this is no different for the people you support. The key difference is that you need to complete a written risk assessment form for their date.

A risk assessment does not prevent a service user from doing something; it is an excellent tool for identifying the possible risks and looks at ways of reducing the potential hazards.

- Look for hazards.
- Look at the likelihood for this to cause harm to a person.
- Look at the severity of the harm and/or damage.
- Look to see what control measures you have in place.
- The risks will need to be managed and safeguards will need to be put in place to enable the service user to be an equal in the relationship.

You will not be completing this risk assessment alone. You will do it with the manager and, where possible, the service user. Your manager may wish to involve others in this, perhaps the family, the community nurse who has known the person for some time perhaps, etc.

You may like to start thinking about the potential risks for the service user and others going to venues where people have the same interests.

✍ I have listed some possible risks. Please tick if they are applicable to the service user you support, and add those that I have not thought of.

| Going to places to meet people who share the same interests | ✓ |
|---|---|
| The venue may be with new people but they do not have the same interests as the service user and the service user gets upset by this | |
| The person does not like crowds and he begins to panic | |
| The service user has limited concentration and can appear bored | |
| The service user can get excited and scream and shout | |
| The service user does not like using public transport | |
| The service user does not like eating with others | |
| The service user attaches himself too quickly to strangers | |
| | |
| | |
| | |

Consider whether a potential friend needs to have a Criminal Records Bureau (CRB) check. Will this put the person off? Who will pay for it?

There is more information about risk and sexual relationships on pp.97–103.

## RECORDING AND REPORTING

It is important to record what is happening in the person's life and this includes trying new activities, wanting friends, and ending friendships and relationships. As mentioned on p.52, it is helpful to timetable events to help the service user to plan, but it is also important to record timetables in the house diary and record in the person's support plan to enable consistency. Should you be off sick one week, then another team member can continue supporting the person, and others can see how well the service user got on and if any changes need to happen next time: e.g. you may have left the house at 7pm and the activity did not start until 8pm; therefore, you will not need to leave so early next time. Or perhaps the service user became unsettled at something and this can be avoided next time.

Recording details of the event also means other staff can have a conversation with the service user about it. If the service user cannot verbally communicate, the staff member can still talk about it with the person. It is good for others to show an interest in what you do!

Within your role you will need a range of skills to be able to respond to each individual. You will also need to be able to write entries in care plans, write reports, complete charts, sign medication sheets and complete other documentation as required by your manager.

You will write down what you have been doing with the individual, also if there are any changes in the individual's needs: this can include if the individual wears a hearing aid and the batteries are changed. You should also note if there any conflicts – for example if the individual refuses to wear the hearing aid – and you should record what you did to resolve the situation.

You should also record things that work well; communicate them verbally *and* in writing. It is important that these things are written in the care notes so others supporting the individual will read it and use the techniques you did. If you communicate it only verbally, it can be forgotten or not shared with others.

Report and record anything that concerns you and anything else that you have been asked to monitor and record. Records are for you to read and for you to write in. Remember, if you do not record it, then nobody will know about it, and you cannot prove that it happened.

You are responsible for what you write and you will sign and date what you have written: this will enable others to refer back, and it can be used in court if needed. The person signing and dating the information is taking responsibility for what has been written. On a practical point, do not use whiting out fluid. If you make a mistake, put a line through it and initial it.

Good recording and reporting is in the best interests of the service user, and is also in your best interests. Below is an example of how important recording and reporting is:

> A woman was admitted to hospital having taken an overdose. Her stomach was pumped and she was transferred to a mental-illness ward where she was diagnosed as depressive. She experienced delusions about Christ, snakes and fire. The registrar gave instructions that she was to continue to be nursed on that ward but that constant supervision was not necessary. Some days later, at the end of a visit, her husband handed the charge nurse a box of matches that his wife had said she intended to use on herself. The charge nurse did not record this in the patient's case notes. A few days later the patient went into the toilets with another box of matches and set fire to her skirt.

> The trial judge in the case ruled that both the doctor and the nurse owed a duty of care. In the case of the doctor, the standard of care had not been breached, but in the case of the nurse this standard had been breached because any reasonably competent nurse would have recorded the incident with the matches. (Aslangul and Meggitt 1996)

A common question I am asked is 'How much should I write?' For example, is writing 'Joe was upset' OK? The answer is 'No'. You will need to write more: when you are writing, you are making a record of what happened and need to give an accurate account which will enable the rest of the team to read it and act on it if required. There may also be a need to refer back to it at a later date. In relation to writing about Joe, you would need to write the time and the reason for the upset, possibly what happened before and what happened afterwards.

The records may be held on the workplace computer. Records on the computer should be saved in such a way that you or anyone else is prevented from deleting any information by mistake. It is important that a computer is not left unattended while the records are accessible.

Writing can be on a needs basis: when writing in care plans for a service user with constipation, you will need to write if they have opened their bowels; others who do not have a problem with their bowels would not require such a note. Instead you may need to record their food intake or what they did during the day. Your manager will inform you on what kind of information needs to be recorded for each individual.

When you need to write something in a file or care plan, you need to inform the relevant staff member that you have taken the file out of the cabinet to write in it. If the filing cabinet does not have dividers saying what each item is, you may wish to put something in the place where you took the file from.

You need to inform the service user that you are going to write something and ask if they want to be with you when you write it, or if they want to have it read out to them once written.

When writing you:

- must write clearly so other people can read what you have written
- should write only facts, do not write opinions
- must sign and date what you have written
- should use the spell check if using a computer.

It is important that you write only factual information. A fact is a reliable source of information. An opinion is a person's version of what they think happened or assume to be true.

- A fact: it is raining today.
- An opinion: I think it might rain today.

After writing in the care plan folder you must then return it to the secure area, whether this is filing in an office or a locked filing cabinet if you work in a residential service. If you are working in someone's home, the service user will have his own place where he would like to keep the care plan.

# Confidentiality

Within your role you will be privy to a lot of information which is sensitive and confidential. You are being trusted to not tell people unless there is a reason to do so and with the service user's consent. The service user or someone on the service user's behalf will give permission for information to be used to provide care and support, and this will be recorded. The service user does not need to be asked again – although you may like to ask him from time to time to ensure he still agrees to it.

As a social care worker you must strive to maintain the confidence and trust of individuals and carers. This includes:

- Being honest and trustworthy
- Communicating in an appropriate, open, accurate and straightforward way
- Respecting confidential information and clearly explaining agency policies about confidentiality to individuals and carers
- Being reliable and dependable
- Honouring work commitments, agreements and arrangements and, when it is not possible to do so, explaining why to individuals and carers
- Declaring issues that might create conflicts of interest and making sure that they do not influence your judgement or practice; and
- Adhering to policies and procedures about accepting gifts and money from individuals and carers.

(General Social Care Council 2002 Standard 2)

There will be times when you may need to share information with others, e.g. a general practitioner, other professionals, family planning, advocate, volunteer etc. You will need to tell the individual that you are going to pass on this information and explain why, e.g. continuity of care and support.

Another example of passing on information is if a service user has been harmed by someone or is going to harm themselves; then you need to tell the individual that you will need to pass this information on. Sometimes individuals will tell you something and say, 'Don't tell anyone, it's a secret' but you must tell the individual that you are not allowed to keep secrets and will have to tell someone.

You only need to pass on information which is relevant, e.g. the postman does not need to know that the service user is looking for a friend or a relationship but the staff team do if they are to support the service user.

An example of when confidentiality could be breached is when a family member asks about their relative. Unless the individual has agreed to the relative having this information, you should not give it out. The family could argue that they have a right to know, but in fact, they do not if the service user is over the age of 18.

Your company should have a policy on confidentiality (Confidentiality of Personal Information 1988) which should cover things like:

- how information should be kept or stored
- steps to take when urgent action is needed
- who will be responsible for deciding when information can be disclosed.

✍ Have you read it yet? Yes/No

If you have answered 'No', please go and read it now.
What does the policy tell you?

. . . . . . . . . . . . . . . . . . . . . . . . . . . . . . . . . . . . . . . . . . . . . . . . . . . .

. . . . . . . . . . . . . . . . . . . . . . . . . . . . . . . . . . . . . . . . . . . . . . . . . . . .

. . . . . . . . . . . . . . . . . . . . . . . . . . . . . . . . . . . . . . . . . . . . . . . . . . . .

## DATA PROTECTION ACT 1998

The Data Protection Act 1998 relates to personal information which can be held about an individual. It has rules that must be followed in terms of electronic and paper-based information and where and how you store individuals' personal information.

The data should:

- be accurate and up to date
- be kept safe
- be fairly and lawfully processed

- be processed for limited purposes

- be available if the individual would like to see it

- be adequate

- not be kept for longer than necessary

- not be transferred to other countries without adequate protection

- not be sold

- not be disclosed to a third party who does not need to see it.

Everyone has a right to access information held on them and this includes service users asking to see what has been written about them.

The individual is not allowed to see any information that relates to him and another person: this information must be taken out so the individual cannot see it, unless the other person has agreed that the information can stay and the individual can see it.

The individual has a right to:

- be informed that records are held on him and why they are being held

- be informed of what the information is about and who has access to it

- have a copy of the information if he requires this

- be informed on how decisions about him have been made.

## ACCESS OF HEALTH RECORDS ACT 1990

Anyone over the age of 16 has the right to see his or her records unless there is a valid reason why this should not happen.

## Code of practice

- Lock records away.

- Have secret electronic access codes.

- Do not discuss with those who do not need to know.

- Do not communicate information to those who do not need to know.

- Records should be handled only by authorized staff.

# Professional Values

## THE PRINCIPLES OF CARE

As a social care worker you will work with a set of values and principles as follows:

- respect
- dignity
- privacy
- confidentiality
- independence
- choice
- individuality
- identity
- inclusion
- empowerment
- partnership
- rights
- equal opportunities
- self-esteem
- image
- beliefs.

You will have received training on these values when you started your career in care. More information can be found in the GSCC Code of Practice and the National Minimum Standards.

We will now look at these principles in relation to supporting friendships and relationships.

## RESPECT

You must respect the rights, choices and preferences of the people you support. This means both having a respectful attitude and using respectful language. You need to call the people you support by their preferred name, i.e. the name they choose to use. If you meet a new service user and his records say Mr Terry Smith, do not automatically call him Terry. Ask him what he likes to be called. He may say he likes to be called Mr Smith, and if he does then make a note of this so all staff will call him Mr Smith.

Many of the people you support will not like you calling them 'darling', 'love' or 'lovey', regardless of whether they have a learning disability or are an older person. The reason I mention this is because many times when I go into homes which support older people, many of the staff use these words and do not always realize that the residents do not like it. Sometimes, the staff use these words because they cannot remember the service user's name.

It is important that you listen to what the service user is saying at all times and show regard and courtesy. This will build trust and confidence and raise the individual's self-esteem.

It is also important that you respect the service user's particular faith.

## DIGNITY

It is important to ask service users who they would like to support them with their personal care. The service user's culture or religion may mean that they have a preference for someone of the same sex; female service users may prefer a female to support them, but take care to avoid making assumptions. If someone shares a similar culture or background to you, it does not mean that they will share your preferences. Some organizations have a policy to say that only same-sex staff will support the service users with their personal care.

Personal care should be carried out discreetly to avoid humiliation and embarrassment. As with being respectful in the language you use, how you speak to people can also help to give them a sense of dignity. Dignity gives a person a feeling of self-worth and affords respect.

A sense of dignity can be provided by being discreet – for example, if someone is keen to have a friend or a sexual relationship, treat it as personal information and confidential unless you are told otherwise.

## PRIVACY AND CONFIDENTIALITY

Privacy is a basic human need and right and everyone has a right to it. The Human Rights Act 2000 states that all have the right to have respect for private and family life, home and correspondence. Circumstances and a person's personality can dictate the individual's level of privacy needed. Here are a few examples of types of privacy:

- being given time to think
- when making a telephone call
- having your post kept private (this is infringed when someone else opens a letter addressed to the service user and reads it)
- having private time to listen to music, read or draw
- being able to speak in confidence: if you know of confidential information about a service user, keeping it confidential will help to build trust and will respect their right to privacy.

**10.1:** The arrangements for health and personal care ensure that service users' privacy and dignity are respected at all times, and with particular regard to:

- consultation with, and examination by, health and social care professionals;
- maintaining social contacts with relatives and friends;

**10.2:** Service users have easy access to a telephone for use in private and receive their mail unopened. (CQC Care Home for Older People Standard 10)

## Privacy in a residential setting

There needs to be a private area where the service user can receive visitors (CQC Care Home for Adults Standard 15.3). Some may like to receive visitors in their bedroom but many may like to use a different area and one where others cannot intrude such as a private room. It is important that you or anyone else do not listen in to other people's conversations.

It is important that you knock on the bedroom door before entering. You must not go into the bedroom if the service user is not in there and has not given you permission to go inside.

It is also important that you do not mistake privacy with leaving people alone for long periods of time. Some service users will want to spend time alone, but some might be left alone because they cannot move from the spot where they were left.

## Privacy in the community

When working in someone's home it is important that you knock on the front door, or when using the key safe system that you call out and announce yourself. Remember to knock on the door when entering/re-entering the room, for example the lounge, kitchen, bathroom or toilet. At all times remember it is the person's own home.

✍ What would you do if the person you are visiting at home to deliver care or support has visitors? Please write your answer here and give the reason for your answer.

. . . . . . . . . . . . . . . . . . . . . . . . . . . . . . . . . . . . . . . . . . . . . . . . . . . .

. . . . . . . . . . . . . . . . . . . . . . . . . . . . . . . . . . . . . . . . . . . . . . . . . . . .

. . . . . . . . . . . . . . . . . . . . . . . . . . . . . . . . . . . . . . . . . . . . . . . . . . . .

✍ What would you do if the person you are visiting at home has a visitor that he has not seen for ages? Do you say that the resident has missed the visitor, or hint that it is nice to see him? Please write your answer here and give the reason for your answer.

. . . . . . . . . . . . . . . . . . . . . . . . . . . . . . . . . . . . . . . . . . . . . . . . . . . .

. . . . . . . . . . . . . . . . . . . . . . . . . . . . . . . . . . . . . . . . . . . . . . . . . . . .

. . . . . . . . . . . . . . . . . . . . . . . . . . . . . . . . . . . . . . . . . . . . . . . . . . . .

Please discuss your answers with your manager.

## INDEPENDENCE

Encouraging the people you support to do things for themselves is very important and you may need to give time for this to be achieved. You may feel that you are doing the service user a favour by doing everything for him, but by doing this, you can reduce the service user's self-worth and self-esteem and prevent him from progressing and developing or maintaining his current skills.

## CHOICE

The people you support may need some help in exercising their choice and preferences. When it comes to the subject of this book, having a personal and/or sexual relationship, there are complex issues that you need to think about and which are explored in more detail later in this workbook. You may need to encourage the service user to choose a person who meets their needs and to caution them against pursuing the first person who comes along. You should respect the right of service users to make choices about their relationships and be sexually active should they wish to, as this is enshrined in the Human Rights Act 2000.

**7.2**: Staff provide service users with the information, assistance and communication support they need to make decisions about their own lives. (CQC Care Home for Adults Standards)

Service users should choose and express their preferences e.g. what to eat, what to wear, where to live, who to have as friends etc.

**12.1**: The routines of daily living and activities made available are flexible and varied to suit service users' expectations, preferences and capacities.

**12.2**: Service users have the opportunity to exercise their choice in relation to:

- leisure and social activities and cultural interest;

- personal and social relationships. (CQC Care Home for Adults Standards)

If the service user is able to make choices you will need to enable him to understand the consequences of making these choices.

Standards 12.1 and 12.2 above also apply to Older People (Care Home for Older People Standard 12).

Under the Mental Capacity Act, a service user has the right to make an unwise decision unless he lacks capacity and this applies if the decision is an everyday one or a life-changing one.

You need to know the person you are supporting and his level of comprehension. For example, if you give a service user a choice when he has never been given one before, he could become worried and anxious not knowing what you are asking of him. Also, if he knows what choice is, but you have given him too many choices, this could have the same effect.

You can support the service user to make choices by:

- communicating in a way that the service user can understand

- not giving too many choices (if it will upset or confuse)

- explaining and discussing the choices available and the consequences of those choices.

If the service user is discouraged from making choices he can become:

- angry
- withdrawn
- dependent on you.

Promoting choice is very important. However, there is another side to choice and that is restrictive choice. This is where it is in the service user's best interest to have choice and freedom restricted. If restrictions are present they must be recorded in the service user's support plan. These restrictions must be made by a multidisciplinary team.

> The plan describes any restrictions on choice and freedom [agreed with the service user] imposed by a specialist programme [e.g. a treatment programme for drug or alcohol misusers]; for mental health service users, in accordance with the Care Programme Approach and in some instances the Mental Health Act 1983. (CQC Care Home for Adults Standard 6)

> Where the service user is on the Care Programme Approach or subject to requirements under the Mental Health Act 1983, the service user's plan takes this fully into account. (CQC Care Home for Older People Standard 7)

✍ Please ask your manager if any of the people you are or will be supporting have any restrictions in place and the reasons for these.

. . . . . . . . . . . . . . . . . . . . . . . . . . . . . . . . . . . . . . . . . . . . . . . . . . .

. . . . . . . . . . . . . . . . . . . . . . . . . . . . . . . . . . . . . . . . . . . . . . . . . . .

. . . . . . . . . . . . . . . . . . . . . . . . . . . . . . . . . . . . . . . . . . . . . . . . . . .

Some service users will be able to make choices, others may not. It is wrong to assume that if someone has dementia or a learning disability, he cannot make any kind of choice. Remember, many people with a learning disability may have been in long-stay institutions for most of their lives and not been offered choice before.

## Supporting service users to make choices: The Mental Capacity Act 2005

The Mental Capacity Act provides a framework to protect the people you support in making choices and decisions. You may have a copy of this Act in your workplace and it will tell you what you should do; for example, in relation to assessing capacity, you should assume that the person has the capacity to make a decision unless proved otherwise. It also gives information on what should be done if a person lacks capacity. Remember that determining capacity relates to the moment at which the service user is making the decision.

If there is not a copy in your workplace, you will be able to view it on the Internet (see useful websites). The Act has pages of information on how to ascertain if the people you support can make decisions.

✐ Please have a look at a copy, in particular sections on:

- Five key principles
- Independent Mental Capacity Advocate (IMCA)
- The making of 'living wills'
- The new criminal offence of ill treatment or neglect
- The new Mental Capacity Act Deprivation of Liberty Safeguards.

## Deprivation of Liberty Safeguards

The Deprivation of Liberty Safeguards is often shortened to DoLS and is also known as the Bournewood Safeguards. DoLS applied to all care homes and hospitals from 1 April 2009. DoLS has its own Code of Practice although the Mental Capacity Act 2005 Code of Practice still applies.

As the title of the Act suggests, the Deprivation of Liberty Safeguards is about not depriving the people you support of their liberty and freedom. The people you support should have freedom to choose, including what they want to do, to wear and to eat, where they want to live, how they follow hobbies and interests, when they see family and friends etc.

An easy-to-read version of the Deprivation of Liberty Safeguards can be found on the Department of Health website: www.dh.gov.uk/en/ Publicationsandstatistics/Publications/PublicationsPolicyAndGuidance/ DH_091868 or www.publicguardian.gov.uk

Please note that at times the Mental Health Act 1983/2007 overrides the Mental Capacity Act 2005 and vice versa. For example, under the Mental Health Act a service user may have his liberty (freedom) restricted because he is sectioned under the Mental Health Act. Under the Mental Capacity Act 2005 it would be unlawful to restrict a service user of his freedom.

## INDIVIDUALITY AND IDENTITY

It is important to see the people you support as individuals with their own strengths, needs, wishes and dreams. Each person will develop a sense of identity and this can be achieved by recognizing the preferences and likes of the person. An example could be supporting the service users to decorate their personal spaces the way they want to in order to reflect their own taste. Another way of supporting a person's individuality is to support their sexual preference for a relationship, whether heterosexual, gay, bisexual or lesbian.

## INCLUSION

You will need to enable the service user to be included in activities and making decisions on who he wants to meet, the type of friend he is looking for, where he wants to go etc.

## EMPOWERMENT

Within your role you will enable the people you support to do as much as they can for themselves. This will provide the people you support with a sense of competence and confidence.

## PARTNERSHIP

It is important to work in partnership with the service user and others as this brings together different skills and you can all work together to achieve the aims and goals of the service user. By working together you can share responsibilities and decision making and gain views and opinions. You must respect the role and the views and the ways in which others work with the service user. This makes the most of resources and values everyone's knowledge and skills.

There may be a variety of people working with the service user and it is important that the service user understands the roles of each person when supporting him or her with sexuality and personal relationships.

## RIGHTS

The right to marry and have a family. (Human Rights Act 2000)

You should respect the right of service users to make choices about their relationships and be sexually active should they wish to if they are aged 16 and upwards. You may be required to advocate on the service user's behalf and challenge discrimination, but you will also need to ensure that the exercising of one service user's rights does not hinder another service user from exercising their rights.

## EQUAL OPPORTUNITIES

Everyone should have equal access to opportunities and access to services regardless of age, race, gender, disability, sexuality and culture.

## SELF-ESTEEM AND IMAGE

Individuals who experience difficulty in being understood by others may feel incomplete and inadequate and have a low opinion of themselves because they cannot get their message across. They may be reliant on others to decide for them and feel disempowered. This can affect people in many ways. They may stop going out in case they meet people who they know and they will not be able to have a conversation with them.

Having an impairment or disability can affect self-esteem. You cannot usually tell that someone is deaf until you begin talking to the individual. Other times, a deaf person may inadvertently do something which upsets another person, for example if they are perceived to be ignoring someone because they do not hear them.

If a person who has been ignored jokingly says, 'Are you deaf or something? I've been calling you for ages, you stupid thing!', it can be hurtful. If someone is told that they are stupid, they can believe it is true and their self-esteem can be affected.

Being different can affect someone's self-esteem. A person wearing a catheter can feel self-conscious about a bag strapped onto a leg. This could make the person feel embarrassed and not wish to socialize or communicate with anyone.

Some health conditions can cause individuals to salivate uncontrollably, which can cause the service user to be embarrassed and not want to socialize. Try to be supportive. There may also be scope for helping them to address the health condition. In this case, the service user may wish to visit the GP where he (or you on his behalf) can discuss the problem with the GP; the GP may be able to prescribe something to reduce the salivating.

If a service user who is non-verbal has a communication board which is large and makes him stand out, he can feel self-conscious about it, in addition to the fact that he has to communicate in a different way from everyone else.

People may not talk to the individual because of the difficulty, which can have a huge impact on self-esteem and self-worth.

## Beliefs

Many of our beliefs come from our past: what we learnt these as we grew up and continued to pick them up from colleagues, friends, TV etc. in adult life.

Beliefs can be determined by:

- the way the person is brought up
- religious experiences
- education
- life experiences.

We may have similar traits to others and do similar things, but we are all individuals with our own values, beliefs and preferences. You will need to be aware that the people you support and the people you work with also have their own values, beliefs and preferences and this makes us all unique.

It is important that people should have the right to continue with their religious practices if they enter residential care. Age can also make a difference: it is worth remembering that people who are older than you will have grown up with different life experiences. Men grow up having different experiences than women. Some people believe you should not have sex before marriage; others believe that you should not cohabit if you are not married.

As a social care worker you will need to be aware of your own beliefs and how any differences in views may impact on your work.

✍ Do you have different views on friendship or relationships from the people you support?                                              Yes/No

If you have answered 'Yes', please list some of your views and/or explain how they will have an impact on your work.

. . . . . . . . . . . . . . . . . . . . . . . . . . . . . . . . . . . . . . . . . . . . . . . . . . . . . . . . .

. . . . . . . . . . . . . . . . . . . . . . . . . . . . . . . . . . . . . . . . . . . . . . . . . . . . . . . . .

. . . . . . . . . . . . . . . . . . . . . . . . . . . . . . . . . . . . . . . . . . . . . . . . . . . . . . . . .

Now you have completed this exercise, you may wish to take it to your next supervision and discuss your answers with your manager.

# Sexual Relationships

The term 'sexual relationships' is a stark one and it is an issue that staff may not feel confident in addressing. I did consider calling this section 'intimacy', but that term can mean different things to different people, and it makes sense to engage with the subject head-on.

If the people you support are people with a disability or are over a certain age, people can assume that the service user's sex life is non-existent. I hear carers saying about older people wanting something more when they deliver personal care and, when asked what they do when this happens, they say that they offer the service user a cup of tea.

✍ How would you feel on being offered a cup of tea when really what you wanted was sex?

. . . . . . . . . . . . . . . . . . . . . . . . . . . . . . . . . . . . . . . . . . . . . . . . . . .

. . . . . . . . . . . . . . . . . . . . . . . . . . . . . . . . . . . . . . . . . . . . . . . . . . .

It is important to remember that anyone and everyone can have sexual feelings and may want to have sex. There is no upper age limit to having sexual feelings and wanting sex. Some people may think that people older than themselves should not have sex 'at their age' and may think of even the possibility as a joke.

It can be very difficult for service users to talk about issues around friendships and relationships, and sometimes there are sensitive or complex issues involved which make it all the more difficult. It may involve something that they have not told anyone else because the information is so sensitive. (I offer more information about complex relationships and vulnerable partners on pp.100–103.)

## WHAT IS SEXUAL HEALTH?

The World Health Organization (1975) defines sexual health as: 'An integration of somatic, emotional, intellectual and social aspects of sexual being, in ways that are positive, enriching, and that enhance personality, communication and love'. The RCN (2000) definition of sexual health is not dissimilar:

'The physical, emotional, psychological, social and cultural well being of a person's sexual identity, and the capacity and freedom to enjoy and express sexuality without exploitation, oppression, physical or emotional harm' (www.rcn.org.uk/development/practice/diabetes/good_practice/sexual_health). Sexual expression is within the law and you should not do anything that devalues, stigmatizes or exploits individuals, particularly minority groups like people who are gay, lesbian, bisexual or transsexual.

Staff members who make the service user feel stigmatized by even wanting to talk about sex make it all the more difficult. You need to be aware of how you react to service users talking about or having sexual relationships.

✍ Take a little time here to think about how you would feel telling one of your friends about your sexual feelings. Think about how the service user would feel telling you and write down your thoughts.

. . . . . . . . . . . . . . . . . . . . . . . . . . . . . . . . . . . . . . . . . . . . . . . . . . . . . . .

. . . . . . . . . . . . . . . . . . . . . . . . . . . . . . . . . . . . . . . . . . . . . . . . . . . . . . .

. . . . . . . . . . . . . . . . . . . . . . . . . . . . . . . . . . . . . . . . . . . . . . . . . . . . . . .

On p.78 you read about beliefs and completed an exercise on how your beliefs on friendship may be different from those of the people you support. Reread that section and ask yourself whether your own beliefs specifically in relation to sexual relationships may be different from those of the people you support. Once you have done this, you may wish to take this workbook to your next supervision and discuss your answer with your manager. As a social care worker you will need to be aware of your own beliefs about relationships and how this may impact on your work.

## CASE STUDIES

✍ Please complete the following case studies and discuss the answers with your manager:

### Case study 1: Mary and John

Mary and John are in their eighties and live in a residential home. They have been friends for a few months and regularly hold hands. As you walk past Mary and John, you see John kiss Mary on the lips.

✍ What do you think your reaction would be?

. . . . . . . . . . . . . . . . . . . . . . . . . . . . . . . . . . . . . . . . . . . . . . . . . . . . . . .

. . . . . . . . . . . . . . . . . . . . . . . . . . . . . . . . . . . . . . . . . . . . . . . . . . . . . . .

## Case study 2: Jason

Jason is 16 years of age and has a learning disability. He lives in a small residential home. When you walk into the lounge to ask him something, you see he is masturbating.

✍ What do you think your reaction would be?

. . . . . . . . . . . . . . . . . . . . . . . . . . . . . . . . . . . . . . . . . . . . . . . . . . . . . . . .

. . . . . . . . . . . . . . . . . . . . . . . . . . . . . . . . . . . . . . . . . . . . . . . . . . . . . . . .

## Case study 3: Charlie

Charlie is 44 years of age, is a schizophrenic and an alcoholic. You are an Outreach worker and see Charlie in town staring at the legs of young ladies.

✍ What do you think your reaction would be?

. . . . . . . . . . . . . . . . . . . . . . . . . . . . . . . . . . . . . . . . . . . . . . . . . . . . . . . .

. . . . . . . . . . . . . . . . . . . . . . . . . . . . . . . . . . . . . . . . . . . . . . . . . . . . . . . .

✍ Now you have completed these, please discuss your answers with your manager.

## HAVING A POSITIVE APPROACH

It may be possible to ignore that a service user may have sexual feelings. However, this is not the right thing to do: you should have a positive approach and support service users. If you don't, the sexual feelings will not go away and ignoring them could lead to problems which you will have to face later. Best to be proactive rather than reactive!

It will depend on the individual as to if he wants and needs support in establishing or maintaining a sexual relationship. If he needs support this should be based on his age, ability and personal needs. There will be some service users who simply want to have sexual activity; others may wish to develop a more regular or permanent relationship – to get married or live with a partner.

Your manager should consider the needs of the service user and the personal and religious views of staff members when allocating sensitive work to staff. You must respect the service user's needs and privacy and maintain confidentiality.

Knowing if a service user needs or wants help in establishing or maintaining a sexual relationship is not always easy. Some general advice on assessing service users' needs is given on pp.17–18, and below are some case studies designed to help you to give this further consideration.

## SOME QUESTIONS ABOUT THE CASE STUDIES

Please respond to the questions below: once you have answered, turn to pp.84–86 to see what you may need to consider.

### Case study 1: Mary and John

Mary is 88 years of age and has lived in the residential home for six years; John is 84 years of age and moved in four months ago. Last week it was noticed they were sitting together and holding hands. Yesterday they went upstairs together.

✍ Do Mary and/or John need help?                    Yes/No

Please explain your answer:

. . . . . . . . . . . . . . . . . . . . . . . . . . . . . . . . . . . . . . . . . . . . . . . . . . . .

. . . . . . . . . . . . . . . . . . . . . . . . . . . . . . . . . . . . . . . . . . . . . . . . . . . .

. . . . . . . . . . . . . . . . . . . . . . . . . . . . . . . . . . . . . . . . . . . . . . . . . . . .

### Case study 2: Jason

Jason is 16 years of age and has a learning disability. He lives in a small residential home and often sits watching TV in the lounge and masturbating.

✍ Does Jason need help?                    Yes/No

Please explain your answer:

. . . . . . . . . . . . . . . . . . . . . . . . . . . . . . . . . . . . . . . . . . . . . . . . . . . .

. . . . . . . . . . . . . . . . . . . . . . . . . . . . . . . . . . . . . . . . . . . . . . . . . . . .

. . . . . . . . . . . . . . . . . . . . . . . . . . . . . . . . . . . . . . . . . . . . . . . . . . . .

### Case study 3: Charlie

Charlie is 44 years of age, lives alone in a flat and has schizophrenia. He regularly stares at the legs of female teenagers when he is out and often comes home in a bad mood shouting, 'I want to have a girlfriend and have sex!'

✍ Does Charlie need help?                                          Yes/No

Please explain your answer:

. . . . . . . . . . . . . . . . . . . . . . . . . . . . . . . . . . . . . . . . . . . . . . . . .

. . . . . . . . . . . . . . . . . . . . . . . . . . . . . . . . . . . . . . . . . . . . . . . . .

. . . . . . . . . . . . . . . . . . . . . . . . . . . . . . . . . . . . . . . . . . . . . . . . .

## Case study 4: Joan and Janet

Joan is a 54-year-old lesbian and spends quite a lot of time with Janet, who is 62. Twice recently you have noticed Joan hugging and cuddling Janet.

✍ Do Joan and/or Janet need help?                                 Yes/No

Please explain your answer:

. . . . . . . . . . . . . . . . . . . . . . . . . . . . . . . . . . . . . . . . . . . . . . . . .

. . . . . . . . . . . . . . . . . . . . . . . . . . . . . . . . . . . . . . . . . . . . . . . . .

. . . . . . . . . . . . . . . . . . . . . . . . . . . . . . . . . . . . . . . . . . . . . . . . .

## POINTS TO CONSIDER

## Case study 1: Mary and John

Things to consider:

- Age: Mary and John are aged 88 and 84 respectively.
- Both persons' relationship history:
  - Have they both been sexually active in the past? If one of the service users is a virgin he or she may need advice in various areas, e.g. what happens when having intercourse, how to avoid sexually transmitted dieases, etc.
  - Have their individual sexual relationships been abusive or domineering? (If either of these is applicable, the service user may gravitate towards another relationship like this.)
  - Have either been taken advantage of in the past? If so, the one that has been taken advantage of may be submissive and not understand that she or he has a say in what happens in the relationship.

- Are they holding hands voluntarily or is one of them forcing? Check out the body language. Are both happy and the hands and arms relaxed, or is one service user holding the other person's hand tight into his or her own body?

- Do Mary and John both want the same thing (either a sexual relationship or companionship)?

You may like to ask Mary and John casually about the past in general. It may be a good idea to ask them separately and in a private area, so if anything is untoward it is more likely they will tell you.

## Case study 2: Jason

Things to consider:

- Age: 16 years of age, a teenager and has a learning disability.

- Jason needs to know that it is not acceptable to masturbate in public places and should be discreetly encouraged to go into his bedroom or the toilet and close the door to masturbate.

- Look at the reasons why he is not doing this in his bedroom or the toilet. Is the bedroom too messy or not comfortable?

## Case study 3: Charlie

Things to consider:

- Age: 44 years of age.

- His relationship history.

- Has he been sexually active in the past?

- Have his sexual relationships been abusive or domineering?

- Has he been taken advantage of in the past?

- What support would he like to find himself a girlfriend?

- How soon does he want to have sex?

## Case study 4: Joan

Things to consider:

- Age: 54 years of age.

- Is Joan wanting to have a sexual relationship with Janet?

- Is Joan comforting Janet?

- Consider Joan's relationship history, e.g.:
  - Have her sexual relationships been abusive or domineering?
  - Has Joan taken advantage of people in the past?

## Case study 4: Janet

Things to consider:

- Age: 62 years of age.
- Is Joan being comforted by Janet?
- Consider Janet's relationship history, e.g.:
  - Has Janet been sexually active with a lesbian in the past?
  - Have her sexual relationships been abusive or domineering?
  - Has she been taken advantage of in the past?

## DEALING WITH ISSUES RELATING TO SEXUAL RELATIONSHIPS

## History

A person's history of friendships and relationships can have an effect on who they are today and in the future and how they may now react to things. Talking about a person's life history can help to understand why a person is who they are today and why they may react to certain situations in the way they do. You may wish to discuss with your manager before you ask service users and/or their family what their past experiences of making or having friends and relationships were.

✍ Think of two things that have happened in your past relating to your friendships and relationships which have influenced you and write them here:

. . . . . . . . . . . . . . . . . . . . . . . . . . . . . . . . . . . . . . . . . . . . . . . . . . .

. . . . . . . . . . . . . . . . . . . . . . . . . . . . . . . . . . . . . . . . . . . . . . . . . . .

. . . . . . . . . . . . . . . . . . . . . . . . . . . . . . . . . . . . . . . . . . . . . . . . . . .

Discussing past relationships may trigger disclosures of possible abuse. You need to be sensitive to this and inform your manager, who can then make a referral to the Vulnerable Adult Protection unit.

An individual can feel vulnerable after they have confided in staff. For example, if an individual has been abused and is reluctant to talk about it, it still has to be reported and the individual will have to relive the incident by talking about it. They may also have concerns about the information remaining confidential.

## Sensitive issues

Having access to confidential information can be powerful and can be used to inform others in the care team and provide a consistent approach to care and support, but unfortunately it can be abused. Examples of sensitive and complex issues that you may need to discuss carefully with a service user include the following:

- If a girlfriend or boyfriend has rung to say they do not want to go out with the service user any more.
- A bereavement.
- A family member does not wish to visit any more.
- A service user is being abused by his father and you want to advise the person to avoid going home to visit him.
- The individual keeps saying that her 'daughter put her in the home' and she wants to go back to her house.
- If an individual has indicated he is going to harm himself.

Whatever the issue, you need to ask yourself, 'Am I trained to discuss this with the individual or is there someone more qualified to do so?' Sometimes the individual will want or need someone experienced in the above issues to support them through it. Other times the individual may want to talk to someone like yourself who they know reasonably well and trust.

Please ensure the service user has the correct support to enable him to communicate his views and preferences. The risks will need to be managed and safeguards will need to be put in place: the service user needs to be able to be an equal in the relationship.

You will need to ask if they want support from you and what type. If you do not ask you may give support and if they do not want it they could accuse you of interfering or you may give the wrong support, or too much, and they feel disempowered. You can gauge what support the individual would like by asking. As you will have read previously, it is best to ask open questions and in a private area, not in front of others.

There may be occasions when there is not enough time to ask what level of support the individual would like. For example if an individual is going to harm himself, you would follow his risk assessment or care plan and intervene or get help immediately. Some individuals who have mental health needs and who could harm themselves have completed a risk assessment or care plan with the manager or community nurse saying something like 'if I harm myself in the future this is what I want you to do...' and it will have information there instructing staff on what to do.

When an individual is distressed, his behaviour is likely to change from what you are used to seeing. The changes that you may see include the following:

- The breathing becomes faster.
- The facial expression will be frowning or scowling and there is reddening of the face and neck.
- The body language may change, e.g. the fists may clench.

You will need to record the level of support you gave and describe the incident if appropriate.

✍ Please ask your manager what you should do when you are faced with sensitive issues and write the answers here (including any forms you need to complete, e.g. care plan):

. . . . . . . . . . . . . . . . . . . . . . . . . . . . . . . . . . . . . . . . . . . . . . . . . . . .

. . . . . . . . . . . . . . . . . . . . . . . . . . . . . . . . . . . . . . . . . . . . . . . . . . . .

. . . . . . . . . . . . . . . . . . . . . . . . . . . . . . . . . . . . . . . . . . . . . . . . . . . .

## Dementia

People with dementia can experience the following:

- losing interest in sex
- having an increased interest in sex
- being aggressive sexually
- losing inhibitions, e.g. undressing in public, touching themselves in public, making sexual advances to others.

It is important to remember that sometimes a service user with dementia who touches themselves in public could actually be wanting to go to the toilet, or indicating that their underwear is rubbing and causing them to itch, or trying to rearrange their clothes.

Some people with dementia may forget who their partner is or that they have consented to having sexual intercourse.

## Learning disability

People with a learning disability can experience the following:

- losing interest in sex due to medication
- losing inhibitions, e.g. touching themselves in public, making sexual advances to others
- getting an erection without knowing what causes it or what to do about it.

It is important that any service user consents to a sexual relationship, as in the boxed example.

---

A 32-year-old woman with learning disabilities was in a relationship with a 34-year-old man who also has learning disabilities and both wanted to take their relationship a step further and have sexual intercourse. The woman had no verbal communication and used various methods to show she clearly wanted to have sex with her boyfriend.

To safeguard both people, questions were asked about their individual capacity to consent to having sexual intercourse. The man was able to communicate verbally and show he had the capacity to consent to sexual intercourse and it was thought that he was not a virgin. The woman, who was a virgin as far as staff knew, was also able to show that she had the capacity to consent to sexual intercourse.

Neither person was able to understand the consequences of contracting a sexual disease and the man did not have the capacity to understand or consent to having tests to show he had no infection.

---

## Physical disability

People with a physical disability can experience a lack of privacy when wanting to have sex, as one or both service users may need the help of the support staff. Also the moves need to be planned and they may need help afterwards with washing etc.

## Mental health difficulties

People with mental health difficulties can experience:

- loss of interest in sex due to medication
- ill health.

If you have concerns about a relationship which could involve emotional, physical or sexual abuse, you will need to report it immediately to your manager.

## THE PRACTICALITIES OF SUPPORTING A SEXUAL RELATIONSHIP

Supporting a service user's relationship can take many forms, including the following:

- listening to what the service user is saying
- informing the service user where or how to access family planning and other appropriate external guidance
- finding out where the Family Planning Clinic is and/or taking the service user to the Family Planning Clinic
- taking the service user to the shop to purchase magazines, condoms or sex toys etc.
- helping people with physical disabilities in arranging their bodies comfortably
- offering the service user the support of an advocate if needed to challenge decisions.

✍ You must discuss with your manager if you do not feel comfortable supporting people with their sexual relationships.

Some relationships are not straightforward and you will need to check with your manager if there are restrictions under the Mental Health Act or Court Protection Orders that affect the relationship.

Before any sexual relationship you need to consider whether you need to be present prior to the service user meeting someone in order to have sex, for example is the service user nervous or anxious? Also, whether you need to be present after the meeting (will the service user need to talk over what happened?).

While you can provide support you *must not* stray into the area of participation and your home's policy on sexual relationships should be able to tell you what you can and cannot do.

✍ Please now read your policy and list here some of the things you should not do.

1. . . . . . . . . . . . . . . . . . . . . . . . . . . . . . . . . . . . . . . . . . . . . . . . . . . . . .

2. . . . . . . . . . . . . . . . . . . . . . . . . . . . . . . . . . . . . . . . . . . . . . . . . . . . . .

3. . . . . . . . . . . . . . . . . . . . . . . . . . . . . . . . . . . . . . . . . . . . . . . . . . . . . .

4. . . . . . . . . . . . . . . . . . . . . . . . . . . . . . . . . . . . . . . . . . . . . . . . . . . . . .

You must *not* make any decisions by yourself; always check with others, e.g. your manager, an assigned psychologist etc.

## CHOICE

Two people can have a sexual relationship with each other as long as they both have the capacity to make this decision. Capacity is not defined in the Mental Health Act therefore capacity should be interpreted in the light of the Mental Capacity Act (for more on this, see pp.74–75).

## CONSENT

A service user's consent needs to be freely given. They need to understand what is involved and understand the consequences. If there is any doubt about the service user's ability to consent, you will need to discuss this with your manager, who will then comply with relevant sections of the following:

- Mental Capacity Act 2005
- Deprivation of Liberty Safeguards.

Then your manager can call a multidisciplinary meeting where the risks will be discussed.

Other people who may be involved in determining the ability of the service user to consent may include:

- advocate (if the service user has one)
- family or friends
- social worker.

If the decision made is to restrict the service user, this must be recorded and reviewed.

Relatives may have views on the service user's relationship but they do not have a legal right to control it. Social care workers can help by enabling the service user to work with his family to come to terms with anything they may find distressing.

Decisions cannot be taken on behalf of a person who lacks capacity to consent to having sexual relations.

## AGE OF CONSENT

The age of consent protects young people as they may not be sufficiently emotionally developed to deal with sexual intercourse. The ages for consent can differ from culture to culture. The age for legal consensual sex in the UK is 16 for both sexes and for both heterosexuals and homosexuals. It is an offence for a 16-year old to have sex with someone under 16, even if the person has agreed to have sex.

## MASTURBATION

Masturbating may be used by a service user as a way of relieving physical tension. In some cases, the resident may not be able to do this or may want something more. You must *not* assist with masturbation.

## SEXUAL HEALTH

Do the people you support need any help and advice on contraception? Some service users may want advice on which contraception to use, some may know what to use, for example a condom, but may not know how to put it on. Some trainers use a banana or a courgette to show the service user how to put a condom on. I watched an interesting drama on TV a few years back where a young man with Down syndrome sat on the bed of his girlfriend (who had learning disabilities) and put the condom on a banana and said, 'There, you won't get pregnant now.'

It will depend on your role and the training you have received on what advice and support you can give to the service user.

✍ Please discuss with your manager what advice and support you can give to the service user.

Advice on sexual health and contraception can be found at the service user's health centre and the GP can refer the service user to one of the clinics below (or the service user could make their own appointment).

## Family planning clinics

NHS Direct 0845 4647 www.fpa.org.uk

Some examples of what can be provided:

- advice on contraception, unplanned pregnancy

- advice on sexually transmitted diseases (STDs).

## Genito-urinary medicine (GUM) clinics

Some examples of what can be provided:

- tests for sexual and urinary health problems, for example, gonorrhoea, chlamydia, HIV, AIDS, cystitis and thrush

- advice on contraception

- cervical smear tests

- advice on a range of sexual health issues.

The GP can refer the service user or the service user can make their own appointment. Attending the clinic is confidential and GPs are not informed of the appointment or its outcome, unless of course they referred the service user.

## PROSTITUTION

Prostitution is legal in the UK, in the sense that it is not illegal to pay for sex, or to receive money for it. But many of the activities that it involves – including soliciting, pimping, keeping a brothel, and kerb-crawling – are all against the law. (Illman and Newcombe 2008)

While writing this workbook I have told many people that I am writing it and it was interesting to hear some staff views on sexual relationships and prostitution – here are a few:

- 'I think it's a good idea, I am a carer and I support some older people in a residential home and some residents show they would like some sexual activity.' I asked her how she knew this and she said the residents keep telling her!

- 'I am a carer and go into people's own homes to provide personal care. One gentleman I visit wants more than just a wash.'

- 'I think what you're writing would be good for younger people but old people won't need it.' When I asked her why, she said, 'Because they are old.' We then had a conversation about sexual feelings not necessarily stopping as you grow older.

If a service user wishes to use the services of a prostitute there are many things that the service user will need to bear in mind:

## How to find a prostitute

Prostitutes are not allowed to solicit or advertise themselves. The service user may or may not know where a prostitute holds her sessions or how to get in touch with her.

## Respect for others

If a service user lives alone it is his choice who he brings home. However, you have a duty to care and to safeguard the service user so if you know he is bringing home a prostitute or someone who could cause him harm, you will need to discuss this with your manager, who will discuss the risks with the service user.

The service user will need to respect the rights of others, e.g. if living alone the neighbours, and if living with others those in the home, the staff and other residents.

## Other issues

✍ Think about the following issues:

- What does the service user want the prostitute for? Sometimes it is just for someone to talk to, other times it is for sex.

- Safety: is the service user at risk by going to a prostitute – someone he does not know?

- Health: the service user may not know if the prostitute is clean and healthy or has a sexually transmitted disease.

- Protection: the service user should wear a condom if he wants penetrative sex.

- The prostitute could 'prey' on the vulnerable service user and could blackmail him or ask for more money than was agreed. The prostitute may have a pimp, which could lead to extortion by blackmail.

- Becoming reliant on a prostitute: could the service user become reliant on using a prostitute and substitute the prostitute for going out and meeting people who could become a prospective girlfriend, or does he see the prostitute as his girlfriend?

- Could the relationship give rise to jealousy or possessiveness when the service user is aware of the prostitutes' other clients?

## Finances

There may be a financial risk: can the service user afford to use a prostitute? If he lives in a residential setting and his money is kept safe by the manager, does the service user tell the manager what he wants the money for and will he need to ask the prostitute for a receipt?

It can be very embarrassing for the service user if he does not look after his own money and has to ask for money to see a prostitute. If the service user's money is looked after by a relative or guardian, you will need to approach this subject very sensitively. However, it should not prevent the service user doing what he wishes to do.

## DATING WEBSITES

Sites are available on the Internet for people to meet friends, partners and so on. There could be risks attached to meeting people on the Internet and you may need to tell the service user about this. You may also wish to advise the service user not to give out too much information on the Internet.

## ADULT SEX SHOPS

The minimum age to purchase sex toys and adult magazines is 18 in the UK. You may be asked to support the service user to go to the shop or to buy these on behalf of the service user or take the service user to the shop to purchase them. If you feel uncomfortable doing this, it is advisable to discuss this with your manager.

The service user needs to understand that he should read the magazines or watch the videos in private, i.e. where no one else can see or hear them.

## USING A SEX TOY

If a service user wishes to use sex toys there are many things that the service user will need to bear in mind.

- How will the service user use the toys? Inserting an object into the body is dangerous if not done correctly. Staff who have not received training on sexuality and awareness must not help the service user to insert anything into their body or give advice on how to insert it. The resident will also need to know what to do if it gets stuck inside their body.

- When and where will the service user use the sex toy? The sex toy should be used in private and not left around, even in the bedroom, for others who go into the bedroom to provide support to see, i.e. staff or visiting friends or family.

- Cleaning the sex toy: the sex toy needs to be cleaned after each use.

# Sexual Relationships and Risk

You have a duty of care to safeguard the people you support from harm and abuse and you have a responsibility to enable the people you support to do what they would like to do. If the service user makes a decision that has a risk attached to it, the service user can continue in what he chooses to do if he has the capacity to understand the consequences of the risk, but you should never act alone in making decisions or providing support to service users in relation to sexual activity.

We covered recording, reporting and risk in general terms on pp.61–65. The examples below go into more detail about the potential risks relating to sexual relationships.

## CASE STUDIES

✍ Please complete the following case studies and when answering them remember what you read previously on the service user's right to make choices and the service user's capacity to make a decision, with reference to the Mental Capacity Act (MCA) 2005 and Deprivation of Liberty of Safeguards (DoLS), on pp.74–75.

### Case study 5: Robin

Robin is 22 years of age and has a learning disability. Robin wishes to use the services of a prostitute. He lives by himself in a flat. His brother says that he should not use a prostitute as it is wrong. Robin says that he needs a prostitute as he desperately wants sex and has not had sex for some time. His brother says he should not go to a prostitute as they could steal his money. Robin says that he knows this and he will only take the specific amount of money with him.

✍ Does Robin have the capacity to make a decision (MCA 2005)?   Yes/No

Are higher management taking away Robin's liberty or
freedom (DoLS) ?                                                    Yes/No

What are the risks involved?

· · · · · · · · · · · · · · · · · · · · · · · · · · · · · · · · · · · · · · · · · · · · · · · · · · · · · · ·

· · · · · · · · · · · · · · · · · · · · · · · · · · · · · · · · · · · · · · · · · · · · · · · · · · · · · · ·

· · · · · · · · · · · · · · · · · · · · · · · · · · · · · · · · · · · · · · · · · · · · · · · · · · · · · · ·

What can be put in place to minimize these risks?

· · · · · · · · · · · · · · · · · · · · · · · · · · · · · · · · · · · · · · · · · · · · · · · · · · · · · · ·

· · · · · · · · · · · · · · · · · · · · · · · · · · · · · · · · · · · · · · · · · · · · · · · · · · · · · · ·

· · · · · · · · · · · · · · · · · · · · · · · · · · · · · · · · · · · · · · · · · · · · · · · · · · · · · · ·

## Case study 6: Andrea

Andrea is 82 years of age, is a wheelchair user and lives in a residential home. She has sexual feelings and wants to purchase a vibrator. Staff feel that Andrea knows what to do with a vibrator and think that she should have one, but higher management say that she cannot. Higher management say that the service user may leave the vibrator lying around. As Andrea is a wheelchair user, you assume she will use the vibrator when she has been hoisted into bed and therefore it will not be 'left lying around'. Another reason for management saying 'No' was that the resident doesn't leave the home. You feel the resident could be taken out in her wheelchair to purchase one or perhaps buy one from mail order in the back of the newspapers or from the Internet.

✍ Does Andrea have the capacity to make a decision (MCA 2005)? Yes/No

Are higher management taking away Andrea's liberty or
freedom (DoLS) ?                                                    Yes/No

What are the risks involved?

· · · · · · · · · · · · · · · · · · · · · · · · · · · · · · · · · · · · · · · · · · · · · · · · · · · · · · ·

· · · · · · · · · · · · · · · · · · · · · · · · · · · · · · · · · · · · · · · · · · · · · · · · · · · · · · ·

· · · · · · · · · · · · · · · · · · · · · · · · · · · · · · · · · · · · · · · · · · · · · · · · · · · · · · ·

What can be put in place to minimize these risks?

· · · · · · · · · · · · · · · · · · · · · · · · · · · · · · · · · · · · · · · · · · · · · · · · · · · · · · ·

· · · · · · · · · · · · · · · · · · · · · · · · · · · · · · · · · · · · · · · · · · · · · · · · · · · · · · ·

· · · · · · · · · · · · · · · · · · · · · · · · · · · · · · · · · · · · · · · · · · · · · · · · · · · · · · ·

## Case study 7: Trevor

Trevor is 78 years of age, he has dementia and lives in a residential home. Although he has dementia, there are times when staff are washing his genital area that he asks them to do more. Staff say they cannot do what he wants. They tell the manager that the service user has clearly said that he wants to relieve his sexual tension but he cannot do it by himself as he cannot use his hands. Staff are aware that they cannot do anything physically to Trevor as it would then be seen as sexual abuse. Staff want to ask management if they can discuss with Trevor whether he would like to see a prostitute. They feel management would say 'No' as they are quite old fashioned in their thinking.

✍ Does Trevor have the capacity to make a decision (MCA 2005)?  Yes/No

If management say 'No', are they taking away Trevor's liberty
or freedom (DoLS) ?                                                    Yes/No
What are the risks involved?

. . . . . . . . . . . . . . . . . . . . . . . . . . . . . . . . . . . . . . . . . . . . . . . . . . . . .

. . . . . . . . . . . . . . . . . . . . . . . . . . . . . . . . . . . . . . . . . . . . . . . . . . . . .

. . . . . . . . . . . . . . . . . . . . . . . . . . . . . . . . . . . . . . . . . . . . . . . . . . . . .

What can be put in place to minimize these risks?

. . . . . . . . . . . . . . . . . . . . . . . . . . . . . . . . . . . . . . . . . . . . . . . . . . . . .

. . . . . . . . . . . . . . . . . . . . . . . . . . . . . . . . . . . . . . . . . . . . . . . . . . . . .

. . . . . . . . . . . . . . . . . . . . . . . . . . . . . . . . . . . . . . . . . . . . . . . . . . . . .

## Case study 8: Terry

Terry is 40 years of age and has schizophrenia and agrophobia. Terry wants to buy some adult magazines and asks his carer if he will take him on Thursday when they go out to do some food shopping. His carer doesn't feel it's a good idea as the magazines are a waste of money. Terry replies, 'It's my money.' The carer says, 'I am not going out with you on Thursday if you are going to buy that rubbish. They aren't good for you.'

✍ Does Terry have the capacity to make a decision (MCA 2005)?   Yes/No

Is the carer taking away Terry's liberty or freedom (DoLS)?            Yes/No

What are the risks involved?

. . . . . . . . . . . . . . . . . . . . . . . . . . . . . . . . . . . . . . . . . . . . . . .

. . . . . . . . . . . . . . . . . . . . . . . . . . . . . . . . . . . . . . . . . . . . . . .

. . . . . . . . . . . . . . . . . . . . . . . . . . . . . . . . . . . . . . . . . . . . . . .

What can be put in place to minimize these risks?

. . . . . . . . . . . . . . . . . . . . . . . . . . . . . . . . . . . . . . . . . . . . . . .

. . . . . . . . . . . . . . . . . . . . . . . . . . . . . . . . . . . . . . . . . . . . . . .

. . . . . . . . . . . . . . . . . . . . . . . . . . . . . . . . . . . . . . . . . . . . . . .

## TAKING ACTION

If the service user's liberty is being taken away, you must bring it to the attention of your manager in the first instance. Your manager may explain that there is a justifiable reason for why this has happened and may show you the documentation to back up the decision.

If there is no valid reason for the deprivation, you need to discuss it with your manager. If after this your manager is still depriving the service user, then you must report it to your manager's manager. If there is not a higher manager in post, you should contact the Care Quality Commission (CQC) office (Telephone: 03000 616161). You do not have to give your name if you do not want to.

## VULNERABLE OR ABUSIVE FRIENDSHIPS AND RELATIONSHIPS

Not all relationships run smoothly, and this can be down to many different reasons. Perhaps the individuals are incompatible or cannot communicate with one another well. Sometimes one or both people can be spiteful to each other either by being violent or by emotional abuse, e.g. one putting the other down all the time and making the other person feel bad.

## Vulnerable friendships

A vulnerable friendship is where one person could take advantage of the other or, explained more simply, could use the other person for his own benefit, or they could both take advantage of each other in different ways.

Examples of the other person being vulnerable in a friendship could be as follows:

- The service user does not know there are boundaries to touching and hugging and he could be overpowering and wants to keep hugging the other person.

- He wants a friend so much that he keeps buying them cheap or expensive gifts.

- He gets very excited and talks non-stop so the other person is unable to join in the conversation.

- He expects the other person to be there when he wants him to, rather than both agreeing to meet at a mutual time.

- He agrees a time to meet the person and does not turn up (of course, this is different if he is unable to use the telephone to cancel the 'meeting').

✍ Can you think of any more?

. . . . . . . . . . . . . . . . . . . . . . . . . . . . . . . . . . . . . . . . . . . . . . . . . . . . . . . . .

. . . . . . . . . . . . . . . . . . . . . . . . . . . . . . . . . . . . . . . . . . . . . . . . . . . . . . . . .

. . . . . . . . . . . . . . . . . . . . . . . . . . . . . . . . . . . . . . . . . . . . . . . . . . . . . . . . .

Examples of the service user being vulnerable in a friendship could be as follows:

- The other person wants hugs and kisses from the service user when the service user does not want it.

- The other person expects cheap or expensive gifts and does not buy any in return.

- He is always eating meals at the service user's home and never invites the service user for a meal.

- He agrees a time to meet the service user and does not turn up.

- He expects the service user to be there when he wants him to, rather than both agreeing to meet at a mutual time.

- He tells everyone things about the service user's past history.

✍ Can you think of any more?

. . . . . . . . . . . . . . . . . . . . . . . . . . . . . . . . . . . . . . . . . . . . . . . . . . . . . . . . .

. . . . . . . . . . . . . . . . . . . . . . . . . . . . . . . . . . . . . . . . . . . . . . . . . . . . . . . . .

. . . . . . . . . . . . . . . . . . . . . . . . . . . . . . . . . . . . . . . . . . . . . . . . . . . . . . . . .

The person may try to make excuses for their friend's or partner's behaviour and hope that the person will change, but it is important to stress that there are no excuses for bad behaviour. They may also be reluctant to talk about issues which are sensitive. How comfortable would you feel about talking to friends about a partner who hit you, for example?

You will need to inform your manager if you have any concerns, and explain to the service user that respect in a relationship means:

- listening to each other
- telling your partner if you are uncomfortable doing something
- valuing each other
- not challenging your partner's boundaries.

The development of trust in a relationship is encouraged by:

- being honest
- being reliable
- being dependable
- respecting yourself
- respecting your partner.

Jealousy is a natural emotion. It is how a person reacts when feeling jealous that is what matters. If there is no trust between each other then the relationship will not be a healthy one.

It is important that you enable the people you support to recognize if abusive behaviour could happen or if it is actually happening.

✍ If abusive behaviour is happening, please consult your policies and procedures on safeguarding or discuss with your manager what you can do to support the service user. Please write what you should do here.

. . . . . . . . . . . . . . . . . . . . . . . . . . . . . . . . . . . . . . . . . . . . . . . . . . . . . . .

. . . . . . . . . . . . . . . . . . . . . . . . . . . . . . . . . . . . . . . . . . . . . . . . . . . . . . .

. . . . . . . . . . . . . . . . . . . . . . . . . . . . . . . . . . . . . . . . . . . . . . . . . . . . . . .

## Violent relationships

If a service user does not have the capacity to understand what is happening, the manager will raise a safeguarding issue and call a multidisciplinary meeting to discuss whether the relationship is of benefit to the service user, what safety measures can be put in place or indeed if the relationship should end because of the risks to the service user.

If a service user does have the capacity to understand and makes a poor choice of staying in the violent relationship, measures need to be in place to reduce the risks. Here are some examples:

Discuss abusive relationship with service user

Highlight trigger points (e.g. what makes the other person angry, what starts the arguments)

What to do to prevent the trigger points

What to do if the abuse or violence happens (e.g. locks on windows, bolts on doors, panic alarms, which when pressed go straight through to the police station, who to go to, safe house and so on).

Remember that a service user who is being abused by the other person can be either male or female.

# Ending Friendships and Relationships

## Moving On

Not all relationships last forever and this chapter looks at how to support the service user to end a relationship. Sometimes people will say upfront that they want to finish the friendship or relationship. Others may not answer the telephone or return calls, or the person's body language may give you some clues that something may be wrong with the relationship – a lack of eye contact or lack of interest in what the service user wants to do.

Where possible, ask the person if there are any concerns you need to be aware of (it is uncommon for someone to stop a relationship for no reason). It could be something small that you could sort out and the relationship would be able to continue. But you must remember the person's right to privacy, if he does not wish to talk about it.

If the service user is able to, he will say if he needs your help with this sensitive situation. If he is unable to say, you should discuss with your manager what he wants you to do in this situation.

Ending a relationship can cause many different feelings and finishing a relationship is a loss which can cause the service user or the partner to become upset or withdrawn. Some may become anxious and/or violent.

You may need to consider the following issues:

- Can the person break or end the relationship by themselves?

- If they need support, what level of support do they need and who from?

- Do you need professionals to support the person or you in this, e.g. psychologist, psychiatrist?

✍ What things will you consider if a service user tells you he or she wants to finish a relationship?

. . . . . . . . . . . . . . . . . . . . . . . . . . . . . . . . . . . . . . . . . . . . . . . . . . . . . . . . . . . .

. . . . . . . . . . . . . . . . . . . . . . . . . . . . . . . . . . . . . . . . . . . . . . . . . . . . . . . . . . . .

. . . . . . . . . . . . . . . . . . . . . . . . . . . . . . . . . . . . . . . . . . . . . . . . . . . . . . . . . . . .

You may need to support the service user and discuss with them the best way to finish the relationship.

## COMMUNICATION

Communication is very important. If both people can talk about ending the relationship, that is good. It is advisable not to send a letter, text or email as the other person might show it to people.

If the service user meets the other person face to face, try to encourage him to choose the right time. For example, a good time is when the other person is likely to be relaxed, rather than in a situation where they are likely to feel anxious or vulnerable.

You will need to think about what will happen when the other person is being told: is there any likelihood of violence? What can be put in place to safeguard the service user?

You have now finished this workbook. Please list below what you have learnt from this workbook and what changes you will make to your working practice:

. . . . . . . . . . . . . . . . . . . . . . . . . . . . . . . . . . . . . . . . . . . . . . . . . . . . . . . . . . . .

. . . . . . . . . . . . . . . . . . . . . . . . . . . . . . . . . . . . . . . . . . . . . . . . . . . . . . . . . . . .

. . . . . . . . . . . . . . . . . . . . . . . . . . . . . . . . . . . . . . . . . . . . . . . . . . . . . . . . . . . .

. . . . . . . . . . . . . . . . . . . . . . . . . . . . . . . . . . . . . . . . . . . . . . . . . . . . . . . . . . . .

List below the areas of improvement that you need to discuss with your manager (if there are any):

. . . . . . . . . . . . . . . . . . . . . . . . . . . . . . . . . . . . . . . . . . . . . . . . . . . . . . . . . . . .

. . . . . . . . . . . . . . . . . . . . . . . . . . . . . . . . . . . . . . . . . . . . . . . . . . . . . . . . . . . .

. . . . . . . . . . . . . . . . . . . . . . . . . . . . . . . . . . . . . . . . . . . . . . . . . . . . . . . . . . . .

. . . . . . . . . . . . . . . . . . . . . . . . . . . . . . . . . . . . . . . . . . . . . . . . . . . . . . . . . . . .

# Self-Assessment Tool

I know appropriate ways to communicate with service users          Yes/No

I understand the importance of self-image          Yes/No

I am comfortable supporting service users who want
to find a friend          Yes/No

I know how to provide social opportunities          Yes/No

I know how to support the service user to build friendships          Yes/No

I know how to help maintain friendships and relationships          Yes/No

I am comfortable supporting service users who want to have
a sexual relationship          Yes/No

I know what to do if the service user is in a vulnerable
friendship or relationship          Yes/No

I have discussed my professional boundaries with my manager          Yes/No

I know the importance of consulting with others          Yes/No

I have read all the relevant risk assessments (if applicable)          Yes/No

I know the importance of recording and reporting          Yes/No

I know the importance of monitoring and evaluating          Yes/No

I know the importance of confidentiality          Yes/No

I know who to go to if I need advice and support          Yes/No

Signature of Learner . . . . . . . . . . . . . . . . . . . . . . . . . Date. . . . . . . . . . . . . .

Signature of Supervisor . . . . . . . . . . . . . . . . . . . . . . . Date. . . . . . . . . . . . . .

What one thing will you do differently as a result of completing this training?

. . . . . . . . . . . . . . . . . . . . . . . . . . . . . . . . . . . . . . . . . . . . . . . . . . . . . . . . .

. . . . . . . . . . . . . . . . . . . . . . . . . . . . . . . . . . . . . . . . . . . . . . . . . . . . . . . . .

. . . . . . . . . . . . . . . . . . . . . . . . . . . . . . . . . . . . . . . . . . . . . . . . . . . . . . . . .

. . . . . . . . . . . . . . . . . . . . . . . . . . . . . . . . . . . . . . . . . . . . . . . . . . . . . . . . .

# Certificate

. . . . . . . . . . . . . . . . . . . . . . . . . . . . . . . . . . . . . . . . . . . . . . .

Name of company

**THIS IS TO CERTIFY THAT**

. . . . . . . . . . . . . . . . . . . . . . . . . . . . . . . . . . . . . . . . . . . . . . .

Name of learner

Has completed training on

Supporting Relationships and Friendships

ON

. . . . . . . . . . . . . . . . . . . . . . . . . . . . . . . . . . . . . . . . . . . . . . .

Date

Name of Manager/Trainer . . . . . . . . . . . . . . . . . . . . . . . . . . .

Signature of Manager/Trainer . . . . . . . . . . . . . . . . . . . . . . . .

Name of workplace/training venue . . . . . . . . . . . . . . . . . . . .

Date . . . . . . . . . . . . . . . . . . . . . . . . . . . . . . . . . . . . . . . . .

This training has covered:

- Responsibilities
- Principles of Care and Beliefs
- Making Choices
- Human growth and development
- Support
- Skills needed to be a friend
- Professional boundaries
- Planning
- Providing opportunities to socialise
- Social skills
- Positive self image
- Confidentiality
- Maintaining current friends
- Sexual Relationships
- Vulnerable Friendships and Relationships
- Ending relationships and moving on
- Recording and reporting

# Legislation and Useful Websites

## LEGISLATION THAT COULD BE APPLICABLE TO THE PEOPLE YOU SUPPORT

**Care Standards Act 2000**

This Act (CSA) provides for the administration of a variety of care institutions, including children's homes, independent hospitals, nursing homes and residential care homes.

**Data Protection Act 1998**

This Act protects the rights of the service user on information that is obtained, stored, processed or supplied and applies to both computerized and paper records; it requires that appropriate security measures are in place.

**Human Rights Act 2000**

This Act promotes the fundamental rights and freedoms contained in the European Convention on Human Rights.

**Mental Capacity Act 2005**

This Act provides a clearer legal framework for people who lack capacity and sets out key principles and safeguards. It also includes the 'Deprivation of Liberty Safeguards' which aim to provide legal protection for vulnerable people who are deprived of their liberty other than under the Mental Health Act 1983. The Act came into effect in April 2009.

**Mental Health Act 1983 as amended by the Mental Health Act 2007**

This Act makes provision for the compulsory detention and treatment in hospital of those with mental disorder.

**NHS and Community Care Act 1990**

This Act helps people live safely in the community.

**Obscene Publications Act 1957**

This Act relates to the publication of obscene matter, e.g. pornography.

**Safeguarding Vulnerable Groups Act 2006**

The aim of this Act is to strengthen current safeguarding arrangements and prevent unsuitable people from working with children and adults who are vulnerable. It will change the way vetting happens. The first part of the Safeguarding Vulnerable Groups Act came into force in October 2009. There is a timeline for the implementation of the rest of it over five years. The Safeguarding Vulnerable Groups Act 2006 was passed as a result of the Bichard Inquiry arising from the Soham murders in 2002, when the schoolgirls Jessica Chapman and Holly Wells were murdered by Ian Huntley (a school caretaker).

**Sexual Offences Act 2003**

This Act makes new provision about sexual offences, their prevention and the protection from harm and sexual acts.

## USEFUL WEBSITES

### All the following websites were accessed on 16 January 2010.

**Action on Elder Abuse**

www.elderabuse.org.uk
Works to protect, and prevent the abuse of, vulnerable older adults..

**Age Concern**

www.ageconcern.org.uk
Promotes the well-being of all older people

**Alzheimer's Society**

www.alzheimers.org.uk
Leads the fight against dementia

**Care Quality Commission**

www.cqc.org.uk
Inspects and reports on care services and councils and is independent but set up by Government to improve social care and stamp out bad practice

**Change**

www.changepeople.co.uk
Promotes equal nights for people with learning disabilities and provides information in accessible formats, making it easier to understand

**Department of Health**

www.dh.gov.uk
Provides health and social care policy, guidance and publications for NHS and social care professionals

**Deprivation of Liberty Safeguards**

www.hertsdirect.org/yrccouncil/hcc/acswww/acspolicies/mca/dols/
Provides protection for vulnerable people accommodated in hospitals or care homes in circumstances that amount to a deprivation of their liberty and who lack the capacity to consent to the care or treatment they need

**Family Planning**

www.fpa.org.uk
Provides help and information about contraception and sexual health, and includes a facility to search for local clinics

**General Social Care Council**

www.gscc.org.uk
Sets standards of conduct and practice for social care workers and their employers in England

**Mencap**

www.mencap.org.uk
Mencap is the voice of learning disability and works with people with a learning disability to change laws and services, challenge prejudice and directly support thousands of people to live their lives as they choose

**Mental Capacity Act 2005**

www.dh.gov.uk/en/publicationsandstatistics/bulletins/theweek/chiefexecutivebulletin/DH_41
08436

**Mental Health Act 1983 as amended by the Mental Health Act 2007**

www.opsi.gov.uk/acts/acts2007/ukpga_20070012_en_1

An Act of Parliament that governs the treatment and care of individuals incapacitated through mental illness

**Mind**

www.mind.org.uk

Mind is the leading mental health charity in England and Wales and works to create a better life for everyone with experience of mental distress

**Office of the Public Guardian**

www.publicguardian.gov.uk/

Supports and promotes decision making for those who lack capacity or who would like to plan for the future in line with the Mental Capacity Act 2005

**Relate**

www.relate.org.uk

Provides counselling, sex therapy and relationship education supporting couple and family relationships throughout life

**Sexual Health Clinics (GUM clinics)**

www.nhs.uk/chq/Pages/972.aspx?CategoryID=68&SubCategoryID=153

Give advice on sexual and urinary health problems

**Special Friends Online**

www.specialfriendsonline.com

Helps people with a learning disability, their carers, family and volunteers to meet people, make friends and talk to people online

# References and Further Reading

## REFERENCES

Aslangul, S. and Meggitt, C. (1996) *Further Studies for Social Care.* London: Hodder & Stoughton.

Department of Health (2003) *Care Homes for Adults (18–65)* (Commission for Social Care Inspection Communication Standard). London: Stationery Office. Available at www.cqc.org.uk/guidanceforprofessionals/socialcare/careproviders/nationalminimumstandards .cfm, accessed on 16 January 2010.

General Social Care Council (GSCC) (2002) *Codes of Practice.* London: GSCC. Available at www.gscc.org.uk/codes, accessed on 16 January 2010.

Illman, John and Newcombe, Rachel (2008) *Sex and the Law: How Does it Affect You?* www.channel4.com/health//microsites/0-9/4health/sex/sar_law.html, accessed on 14 April 2010.

Maslow, A.H. (1943) 'A theory of human motivation.' *Psychological Review 50,* 370–396.

World Health Organization (1975) *Education and Treatment in Human Sexuality: The Training of Health Professionals.* Geneva: World Health Organization.


## FURTHER READING

Department of Health (2000) *Domiciliary Care: National Minimum Standards* (Commission for Social Care Inspection Communication Standard). London: Stationery Office. Available at www.dh.gov.uk/prod_consum_dh/groups/dh_digitalassets/@dh/@cn/documents/digitalass et/dh_4018671.pdf, accessed on 16 January 2010.

Department of Health (2003) *Care Homes for Older People.* London: Department of Health. Available at www.dh.gov.uk/prod_consum_dh/groups/dh_digitalassets/@dh/@en/documents/digitalass et/dh_4135403.pdf, accessed on 14 April 2010.

Mental Capacity Act 2005 Code of Practice Section 6[4] , available from www.mind.org.uk/Information/Legal/OGMHA.htm, accessed on 14 April 2010.